A step-by-step guide to

Underwater Video

by John Boyle

Thanks to:

John Greenamyer for generously letting me use his macro shots, and for introducing me to Kungkungan Bay Resort.

Michele Westmorland, Jeremy Stafford-Deitsch, Ian Cartwright, Will and Demelza Postlethwaite, Irvin Rockman and Matthew Lasky for allowing me to use their images.

All my friends in the diving world who have helped to make my diving experiences happen, particularly those in my favourite places in the world Seychelles, Indonesia's Lembeh Strait, Papua New Guinea and Cornwall – you all know who you are!

Joe Stevens for his first edit of this book.

Ian Legge for his inspired design work and his advice.

My parents, who having worked so hard to provide me with a good education and career understood when I decided to give it all up to go filming fish.

And my long time dive buddy Fionn Crow Howieson - thanks for everything Flea!

Dedicated to my grandson Joshua Brendan Boyle.

Josh, I hope that by the time you're old enough to read this book and to come diving with me, there are still the wonderful creatures left in the ocean for us to film together.

First published in the UK in 2003 by Circle Books
Circle Books
83/84 George Street
Richmond
Surrey TW9 1HE
Phone: 020 8332 2709

Design Ian legge

©John Boyle 2003

Print
Printed in China for Compass Press Ltd
100-104 Upper Richmond Road
London SW15 2SP

ISBN: 095 389 1968

Contents

This is intended to be a working handbook rather than a coffee table book. So although some excellent photographers have let me use their images, the majority of pictures in the book are actual video grabs chosen to illustrate a particular point and therefore of relatively low resolution.

Hairy frogfish

Fionn Crow Howieson keeping me in my place

1. So you want to be an underwater filmmaker?

So before we start, do you really want to do this, to take up a hobby that will cost you a fortune, drive you crazy with frustration, and make the airport check-in clerk's eyes light up at the thought of beating the week's record for excess baggage charges?

Think for a moment about what you are trying to do. You are entering an environment where humans were not created to go, where to maintain the basic necessity of regular breathing you require a bulky and cumbersome mechanical life-support system attached to your body. Even then your body is acutely sensitive to pressure and temperature changes limiting the length of time that you can remain underwater.

Your senses are confused. You experience the sensation of weightlessness. Your eyes play tricks on you – colours appear different and eventually disappear with depth, you reach out to touch something and it is actually further away than it appears. You are at the mercy of surge, drift, up-currents and down currents, and of variations in the clarity of the water. And in this alien environment you actually want to try and take video footage?

You are also at the mercy of delicate technology that was never designed for such brutal treatment, such hot or cold, damp and humid

Filming sharks – the dream of all underwater-film makers

conditions, bumpy boat rides and long journeys. You are taking sensitive electronic camera equipment into wet environments where it was never designed to go; assembling it in inhospitable surroundings – boats, beaches, your car; lugging it into the ocean after boat rides.

Then there's the impact on your finances. It's not just a question of buying a camera. There is the extra expense of investing in a housing, lights, carrying case, accessories, spares, an editing facility… and just when you think that you're at last all set up and you are at your destination and about to go diving, your camera decides it's had enough of this rough treatment and refuses to work. The camera is now out of production and as your housing is only designed for that specific model the housing itself is now obsolete and you have to start spending all over again.

Forget the days of travelling light and not approaching an airline check-in desk with fear. Twenty kilogram weight restrictions? Your housing, lights, chargers, spares, accessories and tapes account for this without considering your dive gear and clothing. Airline check-in desks

become the stuff of nightmares. You start to look with envy at fellow passengers who are checking in a case of clothes and a light carry-on bag. Your own carry-on alone probably weighs more than their entire baggage as you have crammed into it the heaviest and most compact items such as batteries and lights after re-weighing your bags time and again on the bathroom scales.

And if you've not forgotten some tiny but essential part, if your batteries have held their charge, your luggage has not been lost and has arrived intact with all equipment in full working order and at last you roll off the boat for the dive and see with relief that the housing hasn't flooded – you can guarantee that when you come to set up for that first shot that all the planning, expense, time trouble and travel has built up to, that creative moment that you've been dreaming of – you've probably left a lens cover on inside the housing or forgotten to turn on some minor but essential switch so the camera just won't operate!

Just think about that simple example. Leaving the lens cap on is something we've all done on dry land. Everyone laughs, you look a little silly, but then it's off with the lens cap and you get your shot.

Underwater it's not so simple. Letting your buddy know what is happening you surface, – in itself an operation that plays havoc with your dive profile and air consumption – and return to the boat, which may by now be some considerable distance away. Hand the camera up to a small boat tossing and pitching in the surge, off with weight belt tank mask and fins and climb back on board. Off with gloves and hood, get dry yourself and then try and find a dry covered area on the boat to open up the housing, making sure that no drips whatsoever can get in – the slightest drops of moisture can at best cause condensation and at worst irreparably damage the sensitive electronics of camera and housing. And a dive boat at sea is never the optimum place to work on a camera! To get to the lens cap you will probably have to remove the camera from the housing, disconnecting cables as you go. Remove the lens cap and reverse the procedure – reassemble the housing, kit up, and return to the water to resume your dive – hoping that this time you've got it right, that the housing is securely shut with no loose wires, hairs or grains of sand affecting the integrity of the O-ring as most mistakes are made when working under stress in such conditions rather than in calm pre-dive preparation. And if you do manage to find your buddy again you've used most of your air already. Underwater filming is not as easy as the polished television documentaries might suggest!

But it's probably too late for me to warn you of all these pitfalls – the fact you're reading this means that you're already committed. So, if I've still not managed to persuade you that taking up underwater filming is some form of untreatable insanty then read on – learn from my mistakes and maybe your road will be made a little easier.

And it really is worth it, because despite all the expense and frustration, using a video camera underwater is a totally satisfying hobby, the pleasures that you will gain are immense, and you'll probably never dive again without your camera. So good luck and good filming!

Clownfish and anemone: a classic shot

Rhinopias

2. My story so far

What a terrible waste of a life — never to have even ventured down the corridor that leads to the door that opens onto the perfumed garden. That's my version of something I read a long time ago, and although perfumed may not be the phrase that immediately springs to mind after wearing the same wetsuit for a month, the sentiment is right.

It is easy never to go down the corridor to underwater video, maybe on the basis that it is too expensive, or too difficult. Yet today it is easier than ever to take up this engrossing pastime. Manufacturers produce housings to fit most video cameras bought on the domestic market, specialist lights are easily available, and help and advice are readily accessible if you look for it. A far cry from the pioneers of underwater filming like Hans and Lotte Haas, who while diving was still in its infancy travelled to places where no diving infrastructure existed and experimented with huge film cameras for which they had to make housings and accessories before taking them underwater.

I was one of those people who watched underwater documentaries on television with awe and wonder, but never for a moment dreamt that I could also produce underwater films. The gap between the film maker and me seemed unbridgeable, and there was no career structure to enter into that would lead to being an underwater cameraman and film maker. So how did I get started?

I began diving at the age of 17 in County Kerry, southwest Ireland at the beginning of the Seventies. That first plunge through the green opaque surface of the Atlantic Ocean to see what lay below had enthralled me. In those days there were rich scallop beds in shallow sandy bays, crayfish in such numbers that the illegal fishermen who used scuba to catch them were bringing up two sacks full on a single dive. Huge pollack, wrasse, ling, conger eels and schools of smaller fish were there on every dive.

I have no background nor training in the television industry. Studying politics and economics at university, I drifted into the law as a career. Two years articles in a major London law firm convinced me that I was not cut out to be 'something in the City'. Lunch breaks were spent browsing over diving and travel magazines in the newsagents. Holidays, long weekends, and any time I could wangle off work four of us would squeeze into a Mini to make the long journey to southwest

Ireland to go diving. I used every excuse to escape work – imaginary crises and ailments such as dying relatives, family problems, stress, recurring back injury. It came as no surprise that when I eventually qualified I was not offered a job.

So when I left London behind and headed for Cornwall it was the ocean calling, not career plans in the law. I had taken a job with a small firm of lawyers in a fishing village, work as different from the grind of a big city firm as can be imagined. I could dive after work and at weekends, make a few extra pounds recovering lost lobster pots and freeing up fouled propellers. I was surprised to discover that I was enjoying my job in the local magistrates courts, defending and prosecuting everything from farming and fisheries cases to murders and rapes - dealing with real people and their affairs, not huge corporations. Soon I had my own practice with lawyers working for me, a massive caseload and an equally impressive income, yet I was still looking for my escape. I could go on like this and

Me in my early days in Cornwall

become extremely rich but if I didn't die of a heart attack or become an alcoholic, I knew that I would look back on my life and realise how much I had missed. The words of my favourite poem were never far from my thoughts:

A man with too little has never enough
And daily must strive after more
But a man with enough has more than enough
And should daily give thanks for his share

I once had too little but now I've enough
And that's more than enough for me
If you have too little I wish you the same
And a life that's tranquil and free

But if you have enough, but it isn't enough
And desperately strive after more,
Then I wish you well in your restless hell,
But you'll get nothing more from me

Anonymous

I started looking around and was amazed to find that companies were actually producing housings that would allow you to take a domestic video camera underwater, though in the late eighties this industry was still in its infancy. With no knowledge whatsoever of what I was doing, I took the plunge – opened the door to the perfumed garden!

At the time my surfer son Nik was 12 years old and the house was always full of surfer kids watching surf videos that had no story and were little more than a series of great images set to good rock music – very different to the underwater films that were screened at the time that followed very closely the classic narrated documentary style with serious subdued voices telling a story of danger and peril in the deep. So I decided to make a dive video that actually made diving, like surfing seem fun – driving round a tropical island in an open top jeep to local rock music while searching for the perfect dive.

Ribbon eel

Armed with my first Hi-8 camera, and a housing that was little more than a length of pipe with levers that would catch the camera controls inside, I headed off to visit a friend in the Cayman Islands. In the warm clear Caribbean waters catching the images was easy, and the techniques of underwater filming not hard to discover. However, back in the UK when I proudly took my footage to a small local film company who specialised in making surfing and watersports films, I discovered just how much I had to learn about putting together a film. Maybe I had some okay fish portraits, but how would we link the shots and tell the story - and what was the story? There needs to be far more than just a string of images to make a film. What about cutaways, sequences, and other technical things that I had never heard of? What about a theme – a story or thread to link together all those disjointed and unconnected images?

I returned to Cayman and filled in the gaps. Back home again and 'Caymania' was created. The plan had always been to make Caymania as a video that may sell a few hundred copies through dive shops and magazines in the same way surfing, snowboarding and skateboarding videos seemed to sell. But in the edit studio I came across a television industry yearbook that had listings of a species of human being that till then I had not known existed, 'television agents' who make their business selling programmes to television stations around the world. I sent video copies of Caymania to about twenty of the likeliest who appeared interested in wildlife documentaries, and three expressed an interest. With no knowledge at all about the market I chose the one who had written the nicest letter. Six months later I received my first sales notification – Cyprus Television had bought Caymania for the grand sum of $250 – less of course the agent's 30% commission. But the money meant nothing – I was in the underwater documentary business!

Enthused by this success, I decided to try and make something a little more traditional. At the time the buzz in the dive world was a tiny island in the eastern Pacific off Costa Rica, which was reputed to have amazing shark and pelagic action. I made two trips there and my second film, Treasures of Cocos Island, was one of the first

films produced at Cocos and was picked up by Discovery Channel in the USA.

There have been many highs and a few lows since then. Low points have included seemingly insoluble equipment disasters in the remotest spots on the ocean, excess baggage charges that have felt like highway robbery, and being dragged through a court case – fortunately successful for me – against someone to contest their unfounded claims to rights in my footage but these are forgotten when balanced against the many wonderful experiences.

No feeling is better than the excitement of surfacing from a dive having shot a rare creature or unique and unexpected behaviour. I've met some of the great names past and present in the dive world, dived in some of the most amazing places and encountered creatures that I had never dreamt existed. And there have been many adventures along the way, including dinner alone with all 86 Miss World contestants, and producing Party Political broadcasts in a language that I do not speak for the longest ruling African head of state, but these are stories I'll tell you if one day we meet on a dive trip.

Well over a decade later, Caymania is still selling to television stations around the world. Despite having been filmed on Hi-8, it still remains one of my favourite films. As I have gone on to make more films, I have learnt so much since those early days, had many disasters and made many expensive mistakes. I've also had incredible fun, and sold the law firm so I can focus my energies totally on film making.

Thirteen years on and 14 films later the purpose of this book is to share the lessons I have learned.

Caymania: still selling after all these years

Fionn Crow Howieson

I said there is no career structure for would-be underwater film makers to follow, and my assistant Fionn's story illustrates this. At about the same time that I found myself bringing my ten year old son Nik up on my own, Fionn's mother Carol found herself in a similar position with two sons a couple of years younger than Nik, and as a result we ended up like an extended family.

By the mid-nineties Nik had already been on a couple of diving trips with me to the Red Sea and Cayman Islands, and was booked to come on a filming trip with me to Palau – but he had other ideas. He was 17 by then with a steady girlfriend. Faced with the choice between three weeks diving me or three weeks with his girlfriend in an empty house he suddenly developed an ear infection a week before we were due to leave

and announced he couldn't make the trip. Fionn was 16 at the time and the chance to spend 3 weeks out of school was too tempting, so asked if he could go along and I agreed. After certifying as a diver in the 5 days before he left, thanks to Steve at Cornish Diving, Fionn's first dives were on Blue Corner in Palau with the strict instruction – "stay within touching distance of my right shoulder at all times and don't move from there so I can concentrate on filming and still know where you are". But by the end of the first week he was using the camera, and by the next trip, which was to Papua New Guinea, just he and I travelled and he was jointly credited with me for camera work. By the time he left school at 17 there was no question of where his career lay.

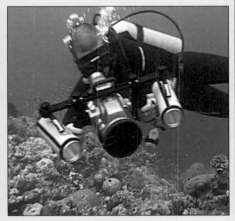

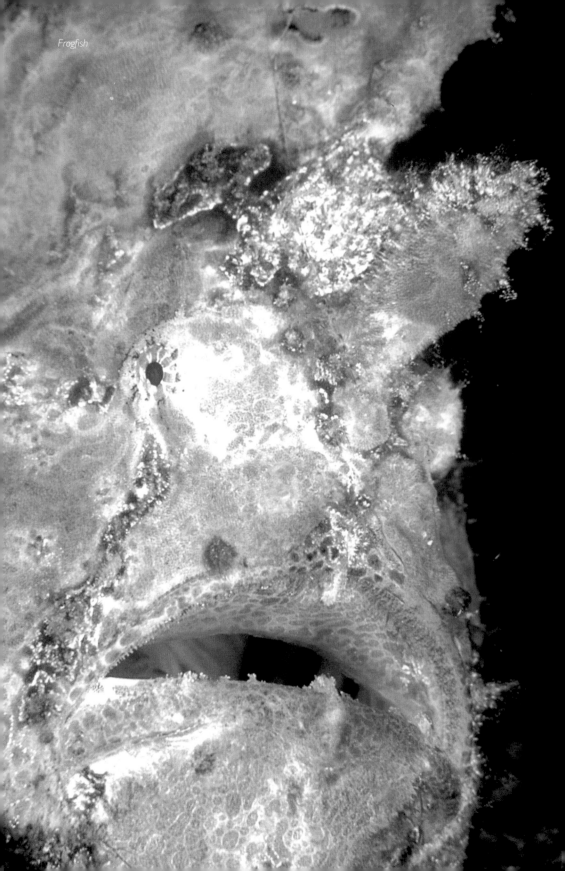
Frogfish

3. Getting started

Why are you doing this? What is your aim in getting involved in underwater video? These are the questions that you must answer before investing in underwater filming equipment.

For most people, the answer will be to take home images from diving trips to remember the dives and maybe share with friends. You are doing this just for fun. When you get home you plan on doing nothing with the camera tapes except having an occasional look at them to bring back the good times.

If that is your intention then that's great – too often everything we do has to have a purpose. There is absolutely nothing wrong with just taking images for the pure joy of doing so. There is no such thing as 'wasting film' provided you got pleasure from shooting it. Sometimes when working professionally it is easy to forget this fact.

When on an assignment it's always pressure, whether real or self-imposed – get in the water as often as you can for as long as you can in the hope of getting that perfect image or capturing that unusual behaviour. It was only recently on a trip to Indonesia with no mission and no film project to work for that I rediscovered taking shots purely for fun – shots I will never use commercially but that gave me a lot of pleasure to take, settling down by anemone for a whole dive, watching the behaviour patterns of its residents – an anemone fish, shrimp, porcelain crab – watching them feed, mate care for their eggs, observing the interaction between the different species.

Nudibranch

This is what filming does – it focuses you. One diver was adamant that she would never take a camera underwater because she would be preoccupied with filming and would miss too much. I lent her my spare housing for a couple of dives and she has now bought herself a housing. Because quite the opposite to what you may expect, far from distracting you from what is underwater, when filming you tend to spend longer with a subject and as a result see more behaviour, observe more, and so learn more about the underwater world than if simply swimming about.

The camera makes you stay longer and as a result see things that you would just have swum past unaware. Few people would spend a whole dive alongside a small coral head in 5m of water. However, I've often done that in order to get a shot of a specific creature, and the longer I stayed and the more I started to see, the more I realised that what had at first appeared an uninteresting lump of coral was in fact a thriving and fascinating undersea community.

Maybe you're a little more ambitious, and plan to edit the tapes into a short film to show to friends, the dive club, or give presentations locally. You may plan to post clips on your website.

Maybe you want to go one step further and try to build up a library of footage in the hope of selling shots from time to time. You may be aiming to achieve a level of ability that enables you to offer to do promotional films for dive operations, hotels and live aboard dive boats in return either for payment or free trips.

You may be a dive shop or instructor considering filming your divers and selling them video tapes of their dives with you. This can turn into a very lucrative sideline and quickly repay the investment in the equipment.

You could be planning to produce a film for entry into a film contest on a purely amateur basis. Or maybe you would like to have a go at putting together a film or video for commercial reasons. Whatever your intentions, there have been substantial technological advances over recent years and excellent quality equipment is available at very reasonable prices.

The first decision to be made is how much to spend and here I have two apparently contradictory pieces of advice. Don't spend more than you have to, and always spend just that bit more than you intended otherwise you may regret it! In fact you can follow both rules.

If you're just doing this for fun, then there are

some excellent small housings and cameras that will achieve everything you could possibly need, and you will be delighted with the results that you obtain. You may be able to buy a cheaper outfit that does not have all the features of the more expensive systems. You will use it a couple of times a year on your diving holiday, and for the rest of the year will have a video camera for general use. Easy to use, light to carry and transport, the camera, housing and accessories will not involve you in excess baggage demands, and are compact enough to fit in your luggage.

I have seen people struggling through tropical airports and on dive boats with heavy and awkward full professional film rigs that have been oversold to them by a camera shop. Usually the equipment is far more than they really need. They would have had far more fun and possibly got far better results with simpler and easier to use equipment.

If you are planning to do more than just take holiday footage, then always go the next stage up – don't ever buy something just because it's cheaper, as you'll regret the decision from the moment you leave the store. If you really want a particular system, or can see that it offers more than a cheaper alternative, then spend that extra bit of cash. It may hurt at the time, but you won't regret it. There's nothing worse than standing next to someone working at a camera bench or on a dive boat, staring enviously at the housing you almost bought and being told just how good it is.

When you have decided which category you fall into, take as much advice as you can.

Most cameras and housings have been reviewed at some stage in dive magazines and there may be reprints on the web. While reading reviews before you have owned and used a camera can be some help, they can also be confusing as it is only with hands-on experience that the reviewer's comments take on any real meaning.

Reviewers may also be cautious not to upset the manufacturer or dealer of the particular model as they are a long term source of advertising revenue for the magazine, so the review may focus on the positive aspects of the product rather than the negative. In fairness the reviewer may not have worked with the housing over an extended period, their review having been done on the basis of a couple of dives with the equipment. Only with familiarity over a period of time when you try and use the housing in differing circumstances do faults become apparent. Having bought a housing produced by a very well known manufacturer that had received excellent reviews, by the end of an extended filming trip I had a list of approaching twenty design faults ranging from poor quality fittings that simply broke or failed after relatively few uses through to major, and basic, design flaws that seriously limited my ability to film in certain circumstances using the housing.

When booking ski trips I have learnt to read between the lines of the tour company brochures. 'Conveniently positioned for the ski shuttle bus' means that your hotel is a long way from the slopes and probably also from the resort itself. Likewise learn to read between the lines of equipment reviews in magazines and on the internet.

More useful is when a magazine produces a table of comparisons of the features and capabilities of similar cameras for a particular model of housing. Careful study of these can be very informative.

Phone around as many specialist shops and dealers as you can. Take every chance to see the units yourself – dive shows are a good opportunity for this. Don't be embarrassed to follow up contacts in the dive world who have first-hand experience of owning and using cameras underwater. Most professionals in the field have been in the same position themselves and are happy to give advice and point you in the right direction – and most of us don't hesitate to do the same before committing to new equipment.

As well as checking out manufacturers' web sites, take a look at the suppliers' sites which can also be very informative. Contact the manufacturers direct by phone or e-mail for extra information – if a manufacturer is helpful that's a good sign – not all are. The results can sometimes be enlightening. If they can't be bothered to help you when you are about to invest in their product there is not much hope of good after sales support.

Anemonefish

4. | Buying equipment

There are two separate decisions to be made – which camera and which housing. The decision on cameras is relatively simple – it must be a model for which a housing is in production, otherwise you will never be able to use it underwater. Single-chip digital video is more than adequate for fun, but for commercial/broadcast work three-chip cameras are essential.

If you are aiming to have the very latest in technology and know that there is likely to be a new camera on the market in the near future, be patient, otherwise your camera may prove to be obsolete almost as soon as you buy it. Also find out from the housing manufacturer whether it proposes making a housing for this particular model otherwise your purchase may prove futile.

Conversely, if having the very latest camera does not trouble you, use the knowledge that the camera is soon to be replaced to your advantage - dealers may be happy to give good discounts on stock they know will soon be outdated.

The decision on housings is more complex.

Buying a housing

There is a wide range of housings to fit many cameras. They range from very basic watertight tubes with a limited range of manual controls that can be adjusted underwater, to sophisticated models on which every camera function can be controlled through the housing. At the top end of the market are the manufacturers who will build a one-off customised housing to your exact requirements.

Electronic or manual controls?

A major distinction between housings is whether they control the camera functions electronically, or manually, by the levers and knobs on the outside of the housing physically touching those on the camera inside. Both have their advantages and disadvantages.

Manual controls are simple levers that pass through the housing wall so that you can press or turn buttons and switches. The advocates of manual controls will tell you that there is less to go wrong as it is a direct mechanical system. However, if there is even the slightest inaccuracy in machining the housing it can be like playing table football and not quite being able to hit the ball. Sometimes the problem may not become apparent for a while, by which time the housing has been used and there can be problems and expense in putting it right. I was recently asked to look at a housing that a lady starting out in video had been sold by a well-known supplier. When she took it back because she could not work one switch the salesman advised her to use a crushed cigarette packet to force the camera nearer the lever. It worked – but pushed all the other controls out of alignment!

A further complaint that I have heard about manual controls is that they allow no finesse in the operation of camera controls. Taking zoom/wide angle controls as an example, most modern cameras have at least two built in speeds of zoom depending on how far the control is depressed. With a manual lever control through the housing this finesse of operation is difficult if not impossible to achieve. While a valid comment this in itself should not dissuade you from buying a housing with manual controls, as in time you should be able to develop a more sensitive touch to the controls and in any event most electronically controlled housings do not offer this option of which zoom speed to select.

Electronic controls are buttons on the outside of the housing that electronically activate the camera controls inside. One clear advantage of electronic controls is that the housing is not punctured by a number of control rods all with their individual O-rings any of which can fail at any time. While wonderful when working properly, electronic controls can go wrong for any number of reasons including moisture, humidity, temperature changes or simply electronic glitches in the system. Once they go wrong, the chances of repairing them or getting parts at some remote dive destination is minimal. You must make your own choice. When working properly there is nothing better that an electronic control system. When it goes wrong you will wish you had a housing with manual controls.

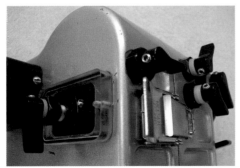

Easy to use manual controls

Electronic, push button technology

What controls are there?

Check which camera functions can be controlled through the housing. Can you switch easily from manual to auto-focus. Can you change the white balance under water? When filming with lights this is particularly important as decisions have to be made sometimes on a shot by shot basis as to the best white balance setting to use – if this is fixed for the duration of the dive and cannot be altered underwater the final quality of shots will suffer.

The more camera functions available through the housing the more versatile and enjcyable your filming will be.

Flat or dome port?

Water magnifies the subject making it appear closer to the camera, which means that to fill the frame with a large subject you have to be further away from it, and the greater the real rather than apparent distance from the subject, the lower the quality of the image. Also when filming underwater, generally the wider the field of view of the subject, the better the image will be. Too narrow a field of view will make it appear as if you have been filming through a telescope! Therefore the general rule will be that the best shots will be achieved by a wide field of view of a subject that is close to the camera.

This result is achieved either by a dome port on the housing or by wide angle adaptors inside housings with flat ports.

The shape of a dome port is specifically designed to remove the magnifying effect of the water while at the same time providing a wide field of view. You can see a similar effect by looking through a fish eye lens in a camera shop, although dome port design also eliminates the fish eye

distortion effect. The main disadvantages of dome ports is that they are not ideal for macro or half and half filming, can be more easily scratched or damaged due to their shape, and generally are not designed in a way that external colour filters can be used with them.

A flat port with a wide angle adaptor attached internally to the camera can produce similar results. Perhaps the ideal combination is a housing with a flat port and internal wide angle adaptor, to which can be added as an optional extra, an external wide angle lens for those special ultra wide angle shots such as the close shot of a whale! And make absolutely sure that the internal and external lens systems are designed to work together without vignetting, which means that the corners of the housing appear in shot. If this is the road you go down, be prepared for possibly very considerable expense. Such external lenses will invariably be a costly extra to the housing and will not come as part of the standard package.

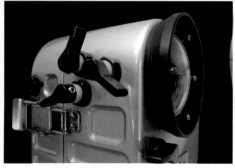

Dome port

An example of vignetting

Can you attach other lenses to the camera?

Does the camera fit so tightly in the housing that there is no space between the camera lens and the port of the housing to attach an extra dioptre to the camera. Dioptres – screw-on lenses that increase the magnification of the camera lens – are essential for good quality macro shots, when you want a tight close-up shot of the eye or mouth of a critter. Yet even many of the most modern housings are not constructed to allow for this optional additional lens

What type of colour correction filters?

Is there a facility for colour correction filters, and if so are these internal or external? And can you choose on a shot by shot basis during a dive whether or not to use the filter?

Internal filters are inside the housing and fall into two categories, those that are attached to the camera lens throughout the dive, and those that can, if needed, be flipped into position by a simple lever movement. The use of a filter must be decided on a shot by shot basis and will depend on a number of factors including depth, ambient light conditions, and whether or not you will be using lights for the shot. Looking through the viewfinder all parameters should be adjusted until the best shot is achieved. If you have no choice on the use of the filter because it is attached to the camera and cannot be removed during a dive, then one option is excluded and the quality of shot will suffer.

If the housing has an internal filter system, check how easy it is to change filters, as depending on the water conditions different filters may sometimes need to be installed.

External filters have more drawbacks. They are easier to lose so make sure they are safely attached at all times – they can be ridiculously expensive to replace. They have to be physically installed and removed, and often when not in use are simply dangling from the housing. They can collect bubbles, not just when getting in the water but even air bubbles from other divers, so should be checked every time they are used during a dive. They can get scratched or chipped very easily, being made of plastic rather than glass. My preferred option is an internal filter system which can be selected as required during the dive.

An example of an internal filter system

An external filter system in position

Bubble wrap

Bubbles on the exterior of the housing port or trapped on an external filter will ruin a shot so regularly check to ensure your housing is bubble free. And if it can be avoided never swim above another diver and through their bubbles as some will invariably attach themselves to the housing

The Golden Rule

The golden rule is never buy a housing if the filter must remain fixed in place throughout the dive.

How adaptable is the lighting system?

This question is particularly relevant if purchasing a unit that is manufactured to be supplied with lights and batteries attached. Are you restricted to the manufacturers chosen lighting system or can other systems be attached? Although the salesman may think this is the stupidest question so far this month, there are many reasons why you need to know. Your housing may have a longer life span than your lights and you will at that stage want to be able to choose from the marketplace. Like me you may wish to attach different lighting systems depending on the type of filming you intend - I use totally different systems for macro to those I use for wide angle work. There may be technological advances in the lighting market that you wish to take advantage of, or the manufacturer's chosen light package simply may not work for you, or may be more expensive than comparable systems.

Adaptable lighting options give the camera and rig a wider range of applications

Internal or external monitor?

Many housings have external monitors which when working properly are fine, but if that monitor fails can you still use the housing – is there an actual viewfinder on the housing itself that allows you to look directly through the camera's viewfinder and is that of sufficient quality? Even if you can see the camera viewfinder this may only be black and white so you will have no idea of colour and white balance if the external monitor fails. A friend with whom I was diving for a month in Indonesia had just such a housing. He was working on his first television project so quality footage from the trip was essential. Only when his external monitor developed a sporadic fault did he discover that although there was a port on the housing that allowed him to see the camera viewfinder, this was unmagnified and impossible to use – for the rest of the trip he was reduced to point-and-shoot filming, and the quality of the shots he was getting plummeted.

External monitor system

Through the viewfinder internal monitor system

Can you attach a tripod to the housing?

Check the underside of the housing – is there a place where a tripod base plate can screw on? For certain advanced types of filming, including macro and half-and-half, you may need to attach the housing to a tripod. These techniques are covered later.

How good is the 'O' ring system?

You will probably open and close your housing twice as many times as you dive with it – prior to dives in order to install the camera and to clean and prepare it for filming, and afterwards to remove tapes or replace batteries. Whether this is a door at the back of the housing or it opens some other way, this is the housing's most vulnerable point for flooding. An O-ring may get twisted or not be seated quite properly, a cable might get caught or a stray hair or grain of sand cause a less than perfect seal. Under pressure water can start to trickle in and cause flooding that can write off both camera and housing.

You would expect that at this point of maximum vulnerability – indeed maybe at all places where the outer casing of the housing is penetrated by controls – that manufacturers would minimise the risk of flooding by doubling up on O-rings. Yet amazingly few have a double O-ring system and most rely on just a single O-ring, even at the principal port of entry to the housing. So check how many O-rings there are.

Single O ring system

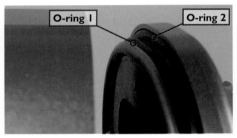

Double O-ring system

How heavy is the housing?

The purpose for which you are buying the housing will to some extent be a deciding factor in the next consideration – the weight of the housing. If you have no plans for foreign travel then weight will not worry you. However if most of your diving will involve air travel on airlines that are not sympathetic to divers, the weight of the housing is something to consider. One of my first housings – which I used for many years when still filming with Hi-8 cameras, was so big and as a result so positively buoyant that it had its own custom-designed lead weight to attach to it – good for getting the housing underwater, but a nightmare for excess baggage.

One working cameraman, who makes his living selling videos of dives to divers at his resort has a housing that he stands on top of to show how robust it is, and that he rightly boasts is fully manual so he can solve and repair any problem that arises. For him the strength of this housing that is used every day of his working life in the tough conditions of a dive day boat is essential. While the camera store staff may not be too impressed if you include standing on the housing among your pre-purchase checks, it is a fact that housings undergo some rough treatment and conditions, and the sleekest looking housing with the flashest paint job and packaging may not always be the best.

Whilst weight does not necessarily equate to quality, be especially cautious of fittings that appear flimsy and lightweight. I have been exceptionally disappointed by one of the most expensive and visually sleekest housings on the market as in daily use many of the essential fittings and attachments have broken or failed. So consider not only the overall weight and construction of the housing but also that of its integral parts.

This does not mean that either lighter nor heavier is better – there are some excellent compact units and some excellent larger ones – it is simply another consideration to have in mind when shopping for a housing.

What are you getting for your money?

Compare what is actually included in the package for the price you are paying. Some housings come complete with carrying case, wide-angle lens, and a variety of accessories that may be 'optional extras' with other housings. Likewise if the housing is being sold with lots of extras you will never use – maybe you already have a suitable carrying case – then see if you can buy a package of exactly what you need. Though 'included in the price' these extras are not free – you are still paying for them and can often get a better price if you go without them.

Make sure you know what the 'complete package' includes

How good will the after sales service be?

Availability of advice and support once you've made your investment is essentially important. If you feel that the person you are talking to is baffling you with sales talk, is not really enlightening you with their explanations, and is being evasive in answering the points in the checklist – then think again about buying from that supplier. If the help you get is unimpressive when the supplier is about to part you from large sums of your money, how poor do you think it will be when you phone up for some after-sales advice!

It is always better to buy from someone who has actually used the housing underwater and has some ideas of the problems. Some dealers are amazingly helpful – call with a problem and they have usually encountered it themselves and have some tips as to how to solve it. However, others are amazingly unhelpful. Buy from a large electrical discount supplier and the after-sales service may not always be of the same calibre as from a specialist dealer. So it is sometimes a balancing act between a lower price and maybe better back-up, though I stress this is not by any means always the case – some of the most expensive can also be the most unhelpful. The lesson here is go with your instincts – you are not stupid, and if the salesman makes you feel ignorant and inadequate then don't buy from that store.

Finally, enquire in advance whether it will be easy to obtain spares for the housing. My own experience as set out below shows just how important this can be.

Info | Check the availability of spares

Though I will be telling you later how after every trip you should fully check all your equipment, I'm afraid I don't always practise what I preach! There is always so much to do when I return home from an extended trip that the equipment overhaul doesn't always get done quite as promptly as it should. A week before a recent trip I realised that I had lost an external colour correction filter on my last trip and never replaced it. No worries, a phone call to the importer should have sorted it out. However despite it being probably the most commonly lost or damaged part, the importer told me they didn't have one in stock. They could import one for me but they only placed an order once a month with the manufacturer and this month's order had already gone in and been processed. They could add it to next month's order, but after delivery to them and on to me it could take eight weeks. And no, they were the sole agent and I couldn't order direct from the factory!

Will the housing take more than one type of camera?

This is a very important consideration. If the housing is limited to just one model of camera from one manufacturer, you may find that it is soon of no use to you. Cameras tend to be superceded by a newer model within a couple of years and if you have a problem with the camera – a fault that is too expensive to rectify, water damage or other accident, or the camera is lost or stolen - then you may also have to buy a new housing.

So check the manufacturer's track record in this respect. Has the manufacturer in the past tried to adapt to progress in the camera market by producing conversion kits to ensure that its housings can adapt to take newer cameras? Is the housing restricted to just one camera or are conversion kits available so it can take a variety of cameras? If so this is always a good sign as it shows the manufacturer is aware of the need to make the housing adaptable.

One camera – or two?

The next piece of advice may sound extreme, but is worth thinking about. Buy a spare camera. It may seem an extravagance, but imagine the scenario: you are on a dive trip somewhere remote in the South Pacific, a trip that has cost you many times the value of that second camera, when your one and only camera develops an electronic glitch – it doesn't like the heat, or didn't enjoy the flight, or it got splashed with a little water. Without a back-up camera your filming is at an end. I can guarantee that the next dive

The camera shelf in my studio

will be the one with the mating mantas, or the whale shark will cruise by.

The second camera can also extend the length of time that you can use your housing - when the camera is obsolete and your first camera fails, the housing does not become redundant because the spare camera can be used in it. Unfortunately, modern cameras are not built to last indefinitely. When a relatively young camera developed problems during the warranty period and I returned it to the manufacturer, the engineer told me that I had used it for far more hours filming than they would expect, and therefore I must expect the camera to have problems! I now have five identical but obsolete cameras for one of my housings, and will only have to scrap the housings when the final camera expires. One of those cameras recently

developed a problem too expensive to repair, so that camera has been sacrificed for parts for the others. Although paying lip service to customer back-up the reality is that manufacturers may charge more for spare parts and labour than the value of an obsolete second-hand video camera.

Most people will want to use their cameras to record both underwater and on land, or on the beach or dive boat. A further advantage in having a second camera is that the fewer the times you remove the camera from the housing the less the chance of an accident occurring. With two cameras one camera can document all your surface footage and one can remain in the housing. Taking a camera in and out of a housing, particularly on beaches, on boats, and in the sort of places divers end up wanting to do it, is a risky occupation.

Carry a spare

The worst will always happen! This picture was taken by Michele Westmorland immediately after I had surfaced from a dive into a previously unexplored blue hole deep in the jungle on New Britain Island, Papua New Guinea – not the easiest place from which to co-ordinate despatch of a replacement.

At around 60 metres, a depth to which I had never previously taken this housing, there was a loud bang and the port of the housing imploded. I have rarely been in a remoter location to produce a film, but fortunately had a spare camera and housing with me so the shoot could go on. Moral of the story – if you can possibly afford to do so carry a spare.

Are you getting the best deal?

When you have made your final decision, shop around. There is no rule that says you should buy both a camera and housing from the same place, although dealers may try and make you believe this. It is often worth investigating purchasing the camera separately from the housing unless your dealer can equal the market rates. Despite video cameras having a recommended retail price, few shops actually sell them at that, offering all sorts of discounts and deals, to the extent that a review in a recent video magazine of a new camera from a major company read: "Hopefully its street price will be significantly lower than its listed price". So hunt for the best buy.

Cameras can often be bought at very substantial discounts from specialist mail-order companies that advertise in camera and camcorder magazines, or on the Internet. These companies buy in such bulk that they can almost always undercut the high street prices. Phone around and play one off against the other. When you have found the bottom-line price that a will eventually come down to, then squeeze a little harder and you will probably find a dealer who will knock off a little bit extra, or who will agree not to charge carriage. In the past I have managed to obtain up to a third discount on the advertised retail price of a camera by intelligent buying.

Be wary of falling for the temptation of buying in an airport simply because a camera is duty free, unless you have carefully researched the market and know it is a good deal. Despite being duty or tax free, airport prices are still generally higher than you can get through a mail order dealer and often even higher than the high street retailer.

Second-hand cameras can appear a bargain, but be careful. Only buy a camera second hand if you are certain of its pedigree and history. There is little chance of getting any satisfaction from the seller if the camera subsequently develops problems – after all, when sold to you it was working fine since then you've taken it underwater – and you will not be covered by guarantee.

Take your dive gloves shopping with you

Most divers don't go shopping in neoprene gloves, but it's worth taking a pair when checking out housings. While in the store the buttons and controls may seem easy to use with warm bare hands, you may want to film with cold numb fingers while wearing gloves. Buttons should be large and there should be no risk of mistakenly pushing the wrong one because they are too small or too close together. Switches and levers should also be accessible and easy to use. The best controls for steady and simple filming are those mounted on the handles, as they can be used without taking your hands off the pistol grips of the housing.

Where to buy the housing?

When buying housings, the number of specialist suppliers is limited, but it's still worth shopping around. Avoid or at least be very suspicious of package deals offering you camera and housing for what appears to be a ridiculously cheap price – the supplier will usually be trying to sell off old or obsolete stock. While bargains and good deals do exist many dealers use trade shows or special offer packages as a way of offloading stock for a very good reason – maybe the camera for which the housing is made is already out of production or soon will be, maybe there is an advance in technology about to be announced that will make this package look very unattractive very soon. Much like home videos, colour televisions, PC's and laptops, video camera equipment, underwater housings and lights often come down in price after first launch as the market moves ahead.

If you are just doing this for fun, it may not matter that you have last year's model; if this is the case with you, then at least be aware that the dealer has a reason for trying to sell off this package – the dealer feels stuck with it and wants to get some money out of it and into newer and more easily saleable stock. Haggle and you may manage to get further discount, or some free tapes or accessories thrown in with the package.

Dive shows are sometimes good places to get bargains on equipment

It is also worthwhile investigating buying from abroad. Even when carriage and import duties are added, if your home currency is strong it can be very advantageous to import equipment. Provided you deal with a reputable supplier, using email, fax, and credit cards these transactions are easy to manage. It also takes far less time than you may imagine to import equipment in this way, often just a matter of days. The disadvantage with self-import is that if there are problems with the equipment it can be very difficult and expensive to resolve, which is why domestic suppliers are preferred by many who would rather forgo the saving to know that they have good local product back-up.

Buying film stock

Before you start shooting there is one final ingredient you will need – film stock. If you buy tapes individually they will prove very expensive. Contact specialist suppliers and buy in bulk. You will always use the tape and the savings are massive. Buying tapes direct in quantities of 50 or more can save more than 50% on retail prices. Searches on the Internet and in specialist magazines will usually lead you to the discount dealers and enable you to shop around for the rock-bottom price. Digital tape stock does not age if properly stored in a dry place away from direct sunlight, so sensible buying can save substantial sums on tapes for your next filming projects.

Info Research the market

Sometimes although the package will look good on the current market there may be a new product about to be launched at a far more attractive price. On one trip to the Far East another diver was surprised that I had just bought a particular model of camera with housing to match. He told me that the camera company in Japan had already stopped production of that model in readiness for a new model – that incidentally would not fit my housing. Apparently the manufacturer was selling off remaining stocks to the European market. What I had thought of as a good deal turned out to be the purchase of a brand new film rig that was already obsolete. My fault for not asking enough questions!

Checklist for buying housings

1.	Manual or electronic controls?	M	E
2.	What camera functions can be controlled through the housing?		
3.	Is there space to attach extra lenses/dioptres to the camera?	Y	N
4.	What type of colour correction filter system does the housing utilise?		
5.	Can alternative light systems be fitted?	Y	N
6.	Can a tripod be attached?	Y	N
7.	Internal or external monitor system?	Int	Ext
8.	How good is the image through the viewfinder?		
9.	Is the weight and size right for you?	Y	N
10.	Is it robust enough?	Y	N
11.	How good is the O-ring system?		
12.	What extras are included in the package?		
13.	How good is the after sales service?		
14.	What is the ease and availability of obtaining spares and accessories?		
15.	Will the housing adapt to take other cameras?	Y	N
16.	Are buttons and controls easy to use?	Y	N
17.	Are you getting the best deal and the best value for money?	Y	N

Buying lights

It doesn't all end when you buy your first housing – you've only just begun! Cynics regard underwater video making as the financial equivalent of kamikaze – and they may well be right!

With a camera and housing you have the basics that you need to take video images under water. In addition, lights and filters are essential for any filming other than distant wide angle, silhouettes and very shallow filming in well lit waters. Here are some things you should think about before buying lights.

Colour absorption

Water absorbs colour. The deeper you dive, the less colour can be seen with the naked eye or through a camera lens, and colours are absorbed at differing rates. In clear water, and in the first few metres the sunlight penetrates sufficiently that natural colours are still visible. After the first few metres the colours start fading and it is to compensate for this colour absorption that lights are essential for successfull underwater filming, not only at night but also during the day.

The first to go are the yellows and reds, and within the first 10m all starts to look blue. To counter this colour absorption the underwater cameraman must use a combination of lights and filters. This colour absorption chart indicates at approximately what depth each colour of the spectrum is absorbed.

Colour absorption is not an exact science. Water temperature and clarity can affect absorption so differences will be evident between warm, clear tropical waters and cooler, northern coastal areas.

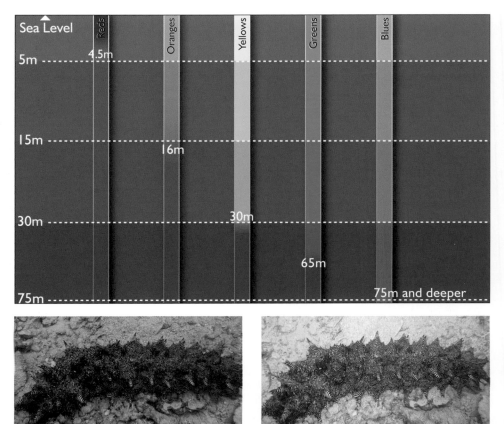

Sea Level | Reds | Oranges | Yellows | Greens | Blues

5m — 4.5m

15m — 16m

30m — 30m

65m

75m — 75m and deeper

A Sea Cucumber shot with no lighting

The same shot with the correct lighting brings out the true colour of the subject

One light or two?

The answer is simple – two. A single light will always cast areas of shadow that will ruin the picture. Two lights when used properly together will eliminate areas of shadow and provide a more even light. Some lighting systems are designed so that both lights run off one power source while in other systems each light is totally independent of the other.

Two different styles of lighting systems but both use two sources of light for maximum illumination

HID or Halogen?

Most systems on the market will be one or the other of these. Generally halogen lights will be cheaper. They burn with a slightly warm glow to them which can mean that true natural colours are not achieved and the picture may have a slight warm yellow/orange tint to it – it will appear to be lit, whereas the art of lighting is to illuminate the subject and bring out its natural colours without making it appear artificially lit. The warm light from halogen systems may not always bring out the true natural colour of the subject.

HID is short for High Intensity Discharge. Such systems will be more expensive to buy, and the expense does not end there – spare bulbs can cost over £150 each! But if you can afford the expense the investment will be worthwhile. They are more efficient in that they produce far more light for the battery power that they consume. Even more important, the light they produce is a colder light, almost white/blue light. This in turn makes it easier to colour and white balance the image and to produce a true and natural coloured image of the subject without making it appear in any way artificially lit.

Integral or external power source?

Underwater video lights come in two basic types – those with their own integral battery power source and those which rely on an external source of power. Those with a built-in battery system are certainly the most compact and easiest to use. Many divers prefer these lights as some are designed to double as dive torches for night diving.

The drawback is that they may be heavy even underwater and cause the overall rig of housing and lights to be negatively buoyant and so difficult to use in many situations. This can be overcome by making your own adaptations to the rig and many cameramen have come up with ingenious ways of improving the buoyancy of their systems by attaching non-compressible buoyant materials to either or both the housing and the lights.

The other drawback of lights with an integral power pack is that they tend to be larger than those with a separate power source. While this poses no operational problems when filming wide angle in open water, it is not always the best system to use for macro or close-up filming.

The second type of lighting system will have the battery pack separate from the lighting heads and there are two ways that this is achieved. Some systems are designed so that the battery pack is built into the housing. This means that the lighting heads are smaller and more flexible, and re-distributes the weight of the power pack from the lights themselves to the housing, but does nothing to decrease the overall weight of the system.

An alternative is for the power pack to be completely separate from the lights and housing, attaching perhaps to the diver's BC, tank, or a separate weight belt. This makes the housing far more buoyant and easy to use, but has the disadvantage of wires trailing between the housing

and diver that can at times create problems, particularly in confined spaces.

If using this type of system there is one more consideration – wet or dry connectors? Wet connectors are considerably more expensive, but make life so much easier. For example, you can jump off the boat with the batteries attached to you and then have the camera housing handed to you and connect up while in the water. You can disconnect underwater if there is a tangle, or to change between power packs when one is running low.

Wet or dry connectors?

A separate battery fixed to a webbing belt

This Y system allows two lights to run off one power source

Fixed or flexible arms?

Because of their weight, larger light units with batteries included tend to be mounted on the camera housing by way of a fixed bracket. Though there are some flexible longer arms for such lights on the market, I find it difficult working with them as the weight of the lights on longer arms can be destabilising and makes it difficult to hold the camera steady for a shot. Fixed brackets that keep the lights closer to the housing reduce this destabilising effect and work fine for wide – angle shots such as to provide fill-in light when filming a school of fish. However this type of mounting system allows only limited alteration in the angle and direction of the lights, making them unsuitable for close-up work.

Lights mounted on flexible arms that rely on an

external power source are increasingly popular. The main advantage of a this type of lighting system is the flexibility it provides in lighting a subject. The power source is usually a battery that can either be attached to the housing, or alternatively is designed to be carried by the diver. Some housings are custom made to be used with a particular type of light, and have fittings on the housing to accommodate the power pack. If the batteries are to be carried by the diver this can be achieved in a number of ways, including on a second weight belt, in a BC pocket, or attached to a tank.

There is no perfect system – consider the type of filming that you intend doing and what you feel most comfortable with. I personally have both types of lighting system and will alternate between them. For wide angle work I use a fixed-arm system with powerful wide beam lights each with its own integral battery pack. For macro work I use small lighting heads on flexible arms with wet connectors to either one or two battery packs, carried in my BC pockets, or attached to a second weight belt .

Left: a rig using flexible arms for each light.

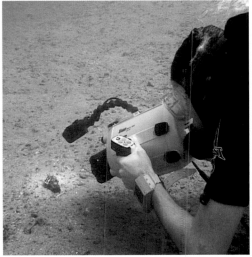

Above: A flexible arm bent into position to capture a macro shot. Almost impossible for a fixed bracket system to achieve.

Angle of beam?

A light's angle of beam is important. Some lights give a wide spreading light while others give a narrow spotlight effect. For general use the wider the angle of the light the greater the spread and area of illumination. However for close-up macro filming small flexible lights with a relatively small spread are better. A few lighting systems allow for different bulbs to be installed giving differing angle of beam, although in most systems the angle of beam is governed by the design of the light itself.

You cannot use a dive torch for underwater filming. Like all torches, they are designed to provide a penetrating beam of light that will illuminate a narrow path as far ahead as possible. Video lights are designed to give a totally different type of light by illuminating a wide flat shallow area with an equal intensity of light across the area illuminated. This way 'hot spots' are avoided – an area of light more intense than the remainder – just shine a torch at a wall and you will see that there is an area of maximum light intensity from which the light intensity reduces the further you look from the centre of the beam.

There are some torches that are designed to carry out both functions and can have a diffuser fitted which will spread more evenly the intensity of the beam. Some diffusers work well, some not so well. The purpose of video lights is to illuminate the subject and to bring out its natural colours and texture, not to make it appear that a light is being shone at it. Ensure that the lighting system you invest in does the former.

Care of stored batteries

Many people will only use their cameras and lights once or twice a year and for the remainder of the time the batteries are lying unused. This can be damaging for the batteries – crystals start to develop which in the long term can reduce the capacity of the battery and even lead to the battery failing. It is always worthwhile to fully charge and discharge all Nicad batteries once a month during periods when they are not being used. If your light is one that cannot be used above water it can always be left in the bath to discharge!

Power of lights

Lighting is an art that is discussed in Chapter 6. Put simply, too much light will overcook the subject, too little will not be effective enough in bringing out the colours. If your lighting system limits you to just one lighting strength underwater then your options are restricted and the possibility of getting the lighting levels correct is lessened. This is not a major consideration in wide angle work when your subjects are more distant and the prime concern is having lights sufficiently powerful to actually illuminate them and therefore make a difference to the shot. For closer work, the need to be able to vary the power and intensity of your lights increases the nearer you are to your subject.

To achieve this, some lights have dimmer switches so that you can choose anything from a dim glimmer to full strength. This is by far the best option, though is usually also the most expensive. A good compromise is a system that will let you switch between two or three different strengths of lighting, which is usually enough for most people. In fact the majority of lighting systems offer just one strength of light; in such cases there is far less control over the strength of light on the subject, although to a limited degree this can be varied by altering the angle of the beam of the lights and their distance from the subject.

Can the lights be charged without opening the casing?

Some systems can be charged without opening the casing of the light. A lamp that does not have to be opened after every use is in theory far less at risk of flooding than one that is repeatedly being opened and closed with the consequent risks of the integrity of the O-ring being breached.

Memory effect

If a nickel-cadmium battery – known as Nicad – is repeatedly used for short periods and recharged before it has been fully discharged, the operating time of the battery will start to reduce. This phenomenon can happen both to camera and light batteries. This is known as the memory effect. While there is no harm done by occasionally recharging a Nicad battery that has only been partially used it is preferable to fully discharge Nicad batteries before recharging to prevent this effect occurring

Does the charging system adapt to different voltages?

There are basically two different electrical voltage systems that you will encounter, 110 volt which is the standard American system, and 240 volt (220 volts in Australia) which is common throughout most of the rest of the world. The difference between 220 and 240 volts is not sufficient to create problems for most chargers.

Many dive boats and dedicated dive resorts will provide electrical supplies for both voltages that will simplify matters but if not, then unless your charger will switch between the two systems, you will have to buy and sometimes carry with you two separate chargers.

Is the lighting system designed to work with just one housing?

It can be very appealing to buy a package where the housing and lights are designed as one by the manufacturer. These systems look good, are well thought out, and both the lights and camera can be controlled by just one set of controls on the housing. Such a system is certainly very attractive when starting out and unquestionably easier to use than some of the more complex lighting systems. The downside of such systems is the very thing that makes them good namely that they are effectively one unit, means difficulties can be encountered should you wish to attach alternative lighting systems, or to use the lights with a different housing.

Mechanical or electronic switch?

This simply means what sort of mechanism turns the lights on and off inside the casing of the light itself. The same considerations as when buying a housing apply. Electronic switches are great when they are working, but if they pack up during a trip there is no hope of repairing them. At least there may be something you can do to repair or at least bodge up a mechanical switch for the rest of the trip.

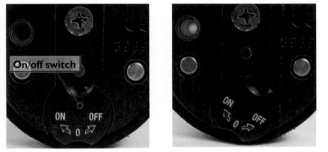

An example of a light switch easily operated with one hand

An example of light controls mounted on housing grips

Is there a safety switch?

When transporting lights you need to be sure that the lights cannot be switched on accidentally. If this occurs, at the very least you will end up with a fully discharged battery. Should your lights be the type that can only be used underwater the consequences of them accidentally being switched on could be far more extreme – at the very least permanent damage to the system and possibly even a fire starting in your baggage! Even if there is a safety switch it is good practice when

travelling to disconnect the batteries – just make sure that you remember to re-connect them before your dive!

An easily operated safety switch will save accidental battery drain

Other considerations?

Apply many of the same tests to buying lights as discussed when considering housings. Are there size and weight considerations that will influence your decision? How easy will the lights be to use in practice when wearing gloves or with cold fingers? How accessible are the controls? How easy will it be to get spares? How good was the advice you got from the supplier and, based on that, how good will the after-sales service be? Do you think you are getting value for money?

Are controls easy to use with gloved, or here, cold hands?

Accessories

Other accessories will greatly improve both the quality of your images and your ability to care for and transport your equipment.

Some housings come with certain accessories already supplied, such as a carrying case. However very often items that are absolutely essential to successful filming will have to be purchased by you as expensive extras, which is why it is so important when buying a housing to establish exactly what is and is not included in the package. Filters and monitors are often not included in the manufacturer's package. Other accessories that I suggest you consider may not be absolutely essential, but may improve your ability to use your equipment to the fullest extent and to obtain the very best images.

Filters

An internal filter system

The correct filter and lighting has a dramatic effect

Lights are not used for all shots underwater. Many situations call for use of filters. Most housings come with a filter already supplied. For blue-water tropical filming, this will be a red filter; for green-water filming such as the North Atlantic or New Zealand this will be indigo. The type and positioning of a filter is a factor to consider when selecting a housing. Some will have a filter inside the housing, others will have an external filter. Whether internal or external, the important factor is whether the cameraman can make the decision during the dive whether or not to use the filter on a particular shot. If this option is not available, don't buy the housing.

If the filter system is internal, check if it can be used in conjunction with other adaptations you may wish to make while filming, such as adding dioptres to the lens of the camera. In some housings there is not sufficient space for both so if you want to add dioptres for macro work you may have to make the choice between the filter or the diopter. Whichever you choose, the shot will be less powerful than had you used both.

If using an external filter, carefully check how it attaches to the housing both when in use and when not needed. Check how easy it will be to install and remove the filter. If the filter will simply be hanging loose from the housing when not in use, this is far from satisfactory. And how secure are the fixings attaching the filter to the housing both when in use and when not? The prices charged by manufacturers for filters are generally very steep and these can be both expensive to replace if lost and probably impossible to replace while on a dive trip so make certain there is a failsafe system for securing the filters.

Tripods

Although not commonly used by divers, a tripod can be a very useful accessory. Small tripods are particularly useful for filming macro subjects, ensuring a steady shot with no camera wobble when working with full zoom and high magnification. Tripods are also useful for filming something from directly above, such as a creature living in a hole in the substrate. Larger tripods can also be useful for half-and-half shots in shallow water.

Tripods are not designed to be used in the sea, and no matter how carefully you wash them after use they will only have a limited life span and will rust out quickly. This is a sacrificial item of equipment with limited uses so buy the cheapest you can.

The macro filmaker's three-legged friend

Carrying cases

Some housings come complete with carrying case. If not, you will need to work out a system of safely transporting your equipment. Any carrying case must be light in order to make transportation easy and minimise excess baggage charges. It must also be rigid to protect its contents, have minimal metal parts as invariably these will rust; and have no fabric inside as this will inevitably hold moisture. Is the carrying case watertight? While it does not matter if the housing gets wet, it does matter if certain accessories such as chargers do. A watertight carrying case can have many other uses so it's worthwhile having one.

A well protected housing

Monitors

One of the advantages of shooting video underwater is that provided you have a good viewfinder or monitor, then you can actually see what the resultant image will look like. Every camera housing will have a small window at the back to enable the user to see

Two examples of external monitors. Note the shades on both

the camera viewfinder in order to film through it. Most will also have some form of magnification in that window so that the camera viewfinder image is enlarged. However this may not produce an image of sufficient size and clarity to produce the best results.

Recognising the drawbacks of viewfinders, many modern cameras now have large flip out screens which when used on land provide a good quality LCD screen. This makes land based filming easier, not only because the image is easier to see and correct as needed, but also because the cameraperson does not have to always be looking through the small eyepiece of a camera. Interesting and innovative shots and angles are far easier to achieve on land using these LCD screens.

The same applies underwater. The larger

the image you can see, the better the chance of correcting focus, colour, white balance, and indeed the framing of the image itself. Some housings are designed to allow sight of the camera's flip-out monitor; others can be adapted or have been designed to take an external monitor. These become essential if the camera in the housing is one that has a flip out colour monitor as many of these cameras only have a black and white image through the rear eyepiece and if this is all you can see when the camera is housed, then all the variables of lighting, colour, and white balance become a total lottery.

The benefits of the larger monitor underwater are the same as on land – a larger image and more flexibility in filming techniques, as you no longer need to have an eye glued to a small window on the rear of the housing.

However as always there are disadvantages to consider. An external monitor is usually an expensive optional extra. Ensure it has its own independent power source, as if run off the camera battery then filming time will be substantially reduced by this extra drain on power. Finally, a good shade for the monitor is essential. In many filming situations sunlight or even general ambient light may make it difficult to see a monitor which is not well shaded.

If you will not be using a monitor for filming, then a small portable monitor to play back your footage after a dive can be extremely useful. Unlike stills photographers, videographers have the instant gratification of being able to view our footage immediately and learn from our mistakes. A shot may have looked great through the viewfinder, but on playback any number of faults may show up. There may have been a mark or bubbles on the lens, focus or lighting may not be quite right, there may be shadow. Sometimes there may be a television available that you can use to view your footage which is a compatible system and you have the right leads, but often this is not be case. Very compact monitors are available that will run off the same battery packs as your camera and which can also be run from mains power.

Try to avoid overusing the playback facility of your camera as to do so can greatly reduce the lifespan of the camera. Purchasing a player for your tapes, either with its own monitor or simply one that can be plugged into any compatible screen, will greatly extend the useful life of the camera.

Spares

While a comprehensive set of spare parts is beyond most of us, certain minimum spares are essential. The following list of suggestions is by no means exhaustive. Make your own list depending on the requirements of your own filming rig, but don't get carried away with enthusiasm. Only carry what you may realistically need; for example there is no need to carry every size of nut and bolt if your equipment only uses a few sizes.

Spare bulbs should always be carried. The bulbs in underwater camera lights are almost inevitably going to be highly specialist, specific to a very few products, and almost impossible to get not only abroad but in anything but the most specialist shops in your home area. Have them before you need them – when you need them it's too late, will always be in the remotest spot and probably at a weekend or on a national holiday when even the stores that might have had them are closed.

A recent shoot in a remote part of Indonesia was only saved by the fact that a friend was flying in late to join us. We'd forgotten spare bulbs for our lights and by some strange twist of fate two of four had blown within the first day's diving. We emailed him just in time for him to pick up spares literally on the way to the airport

Spares list
✔ Batteries
✔ Bulbs
✔ Chargers
✔ Electrical adaptors
✔ Strip of plug sockets
✔ Nuts and bolts, screws etc
✔ O-rings
✔ O-ring grease
✔ Filters
✔ Camera lens cover

Info Don't blow it...

You can never carry enough back up equipment. I wished I had followed my own advice when seriously jet lagged on my first night in a resort, I plugged in my battery chargers and turned on the power – and blew them both. They were for 110 voltage that I was expecting on the dive boat, while the voltage in the hotel where we were staying overnight was 240 volts. We'd not even got on board the boat and I had no way to charge my batteries on the trip. If only I'd been carrying even one spare charger...

Electrical adaptors

Particularly when travelling abroad make sure you have a good supply of adaptors for all shapes and sizes of foreign sockets – universal adaptors are for sale at most airports and electrical stores and are absolutely essential.

It is a good idea to take four bar strips – often boats or even hotel rooms may have a shortage of sockets. Find out in advance as much as you can about the voltage and type of plugs used at your destination and take extras.

Tool kit

A compact travelling tool kit can be put together with spanners, allen keys and screwdrivers of the right type to service the equipment. While most boats and dive centres may be well equipped, you can virtually guarantee that your housing or lights will need a peculiar sized allen key, or a longer than normal length. Don't carry every different size of allen key – get to know your equipment and limit yourself to the actual sizes that you will need.

Another good reason for carrying your own tools is that there does not seem to be an industry standard in the diving world, and both metric and imperial nuts and bolts are used depending on the manufacturer and the equipment's country of origin.

Include a good pair of pliers. These are not just for wires, as no matter how comprehensive your collection of spanners may be, inevitably a nut will strip and this is the only way of freeing it up. Following on from this tip take spare nuts, bolts, and screws not only in the sizes and lengths that your equipment uses, but in some cases also one size bigger and a size longer for that hole that the original thread will no longer grip.

Take a sharp knife, scalpel or scissors – wires and cables all need cutting, and they are also useful for cannibalising spare parts in an emergency.

Cable ties, rubber bands and some string are the sort of things you can never find when you need them, and are ideal not only for in the field repairs, but to tie on any removable part that could either work loose, drop off, or is designed to be removed and replaced underwater such as external coloured filters and shades for viewfinders. Likewise strong waterproof gaffer tape – as a last resort bodge it up and save the day and the dive and do a more lasting repair job later.

Finally a hairdryer – if you have as little hair as me this is guaranteed to raise a laugh – but for getting moisture and condensation out of a housing there's nothing better!

After that list the next advice may seem contradictory – don't carry more than you will need! It is perfectly possible to tailor the kit to the particular tools and size of tools that actually fit the nuts, bolts and screws of your equipment. You don't need to carry a full range of screwdrivers, just the specific flathead and crosshead tools for the specific screws on your equipment.

Always carry plenty O-ring grease and spare O-rings of every size that is used by your housing, lights, and underwater torch. An old toothbrush is ideal for cleaning the grooves in which O-rings are seated.

Tool kit

✔ Screw drivers
✔ Allen keys
✔ Spanners
✔ Pliers
✔ Knife/scalpel
✔ Scissors
✔ Glue
✔ Duck tape
✔ Hair dryer
✔ Tooth brush

Cleaning kit

Cleaning kits for cameras are available at most camera shops and can be used also on the housing lenses. All you need for routine cleaning is an air brush, a fluid lens cleaner, and a generous supply of lens tissues and of good quality lens cloths – you can never have enough of these. Aerosol cans of air can be obtained from most camera stores and are very useful. A head-cleaning cassette for the camera should also be used in accordance with the manufacturer's recommendations.

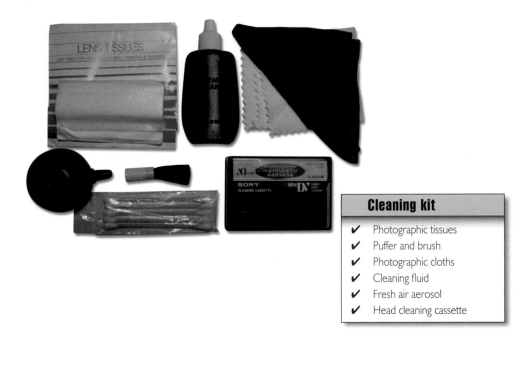

Cleaning kit

✔ Photographic tissues
✔ Puffer and brush
✔ Photographic cloths
✔ Cleaning fluid
✔ Fresh air aerosol
✔ Head cleaning cassette

Checklist for buying lights			
1.	HID or Halogen?		
2.	One light or two?	1	2
3.	Separate or integrated battery?	Sep	Int
4.	Size and weight?		
5.	Flexible or fixed arms?	Flex	Fix
6.	Angle of beam?		
7.	Power of lights?		
8.	Can it be charged without opening light casing?	Y	N
9.	Does the charging system have varying voltages?	Y	N
10.	Can be mounted to variety of housings or are they specific to just one housing?		
11.	Mechanical or electronic switches?	Man	Elec
12.	Safety switch?	Y	N
13.	Ease of use – accessibility of on/off and control switches when mounted?		
14.	Controlled through the housing or independent systems?		
15.	Wet or dry connections?	Wet	Dry
16.	Charging time?		
17.	Burn time?		
18	Variable power of lights/dimmer switch?		
19	Can the lights be used both in and out of the water?	Y	N

Crinoids

5. Practical filming

For the purpose of this chapter, and indeed the book as a whole, I will assume that you are familiar with the camera itself. If not read the camera manual carefully and make sure that you are familiar with all camera functions. Throughout the book I will avoid duplicating information that can be found in the camera manual and will concentrate on the specifics of actually filming underwater.

No matter how robust you may believe your equipment to be, you are dealing with technologically advanced equipment upon which you are relying to bring back first class images from under the sea - equipment that has cost you a lot of money. Always treat it as carefully as you can. A scratch on a filter, a chip out of a lens, a knock to a control, and you could face substantial repair bills. So plan how to look after your equipment at every stage. Storage and travel are dealt with later in the book. I am assuming you have arrived safely at your dive destination and are preparing to enter the water.

The simple O-ring

You have now spent ridiculous amounts of money on a housing whose sole function is to take a highly evolved and sensitive piece of camera equipment underwater and keep it dry. So it is essential that you maintain that housing in perfect condition. If you fail to do so, the housing may let you down and your equipment may be destroyed.

All underwater camera systems whether video or still depend on one basic and simple component, the O-ring. The camera housing is an airtight unit that is taken underwater. As divers, we all know the basic principle that the deeper underwater we go the greater the pressure becomes. Human beings can compensate for the change in pressure upon air spaces within our bodies, equalising that pressure by clearing our ears. The housing has no means of equalising pressures and so the deeper underwater it goes, the greater the pressure of water trying to force its way into the housing. At the surface, the pressure outside and inside the camera is the same. At 10m the pressure outside the camera is double that inside, an extra atmosphere of pressure, and at 20m three times more and so on. One of the most basic principles of physics is that pressure will try to equalise, which would mean a flow of water into the lower pressure area of the housing.

All that is preventing this from occurring is the humble O-ring.

Before every dive it is essential to check the O-ring. The slightest crack or scratch in the O-ring could, under pressure, result in water getting into the housing. Dust, sand, even a hair could provide a breach in the O-ring and cause flooding. If the O-ring is not properly seated in its groove, if it is twisted in any way, then it will not function properly. The O-ring is the thin line separating your camera from flooding.

The O-ring should be regularly greased in accordance with the manufacturer's specifications. This protects it from wear and from drying up and cracking, keeping it supple.

Always carry a spare O-ring as part of your accessories kit together with plenty of the approved type of O-ring grease.

When the housing is to be stored or not used for any length of time, do not leave the O-rings in position. Remove the O-rings, clean and grease them, pack them in a re-sealable plastic bag and store them in a cool dry place. Make sure that they are not folded or twisted when stored as this could result in permanent distortion of the ring, and that nothing heavy is placed on top of them for similar reasons. Then store them out of direct sunlight, and nowhere near a radiator or other heat source, as this could lead to perishing of the rubber.

A single O-ring system can be seen on this housing - the 'thin blue line' between filming and flooding

📖 O-ring maintenance

Be very cautious about how you maintain O-rings and read carefully the manufacturer's advice on this subject. Different types of O-ring require differing types of grease and maintenance procedures; using the wrong grease can damage the O-ring and increase the risk of flooding. Do not use Vaseline or any other petroleum based substance as an alternative to proper and recommended O-ring grease.

Tip | How to clean and grease an O-ring

1. First remove the O-ring from its groove on the housing. IMPORTANT: Never use anything sharp or metal to remove the O-ring, such as a knife or tweezers. A credit card or dive certification card is the ideal tool!

2. When removed, thoroughly clean the O-ring. Do not do this with any material such as tissue paper or cloth that might leave fibres on the O-ring.

3. With your fingers, grease the O-ring with the manufacturer's approved O-ring grease. Note: Do not over grease the ring, just enough to thoroughly lubricate it.

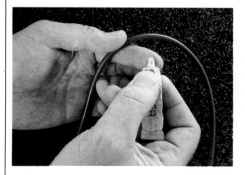

4. While the O-ring is removed, check the O-ring groove and thoroughly clean it in case some dirt is trapped in there. Check that the groove is undamaged, as a chip or scratch will make it difficult for a watertight seal to be achieved.

5. Finally, check the other surface of the housing, where the O-ring makes contact to make its seal, to likewise ensure that it is free of dirt and undamaged.

6. When satisfied that the O-ring is clean, carefully replace it in its groove, ensuring it fits comfortably and is not, in any way, loose or twisted.

7. Ensure, when closing the housing, that the O-ring still sits comfortably in its groove and is not loose or trapped in the housing as it closes.

DIVE PROCEDURE - The ten commandments!

1. At the beginning of every trip or shoot, first immerse the housing in a tank of fresh water and then take it for a check out dive before installing the camera. This way if there is any form of leak the camera will be spared the risk of damage. The same precaution should be taken if you have been working on the housing and indeed before installing a camera in a new housing.

Never leave a housing open

2. Never leave a housing open for longer than is needed to work on it or install the camera. Apart from the risk of moisture and dust getting inside, a stills photographer who left his housing open overnight discovered it taken over by ants the next morning. Days later the tiny insects were still emerging from the innermost parts of the mechanism.

! | **Burning up**

On a liveaboard trip in the Red Sea I could not understand why the viewfinder on my camera seemed to be getting cloudier as the trip progressed. I realised too late, that while the camera storage table on the boat was covered, the angle of the afternoon sun came under the canopy and the housing viewfinder was acting just like the magnifying glass that it is and focusing a burning pinpoint of sun onto my camera viewfinder.

3. If possible before a dive, and whenever you have opened the housing for any reason, always immerse the housing in fresh water, or failing that in shallow sea water, to check that the housing is watertight before committing to the dive. Most boats and resorts have wash tanks for rinsing cameras after a dive – take advantage of these. Leaks can be caused in so many ways – a cable caught, a twisted or loose O-ring, hair or piece of grit or sand, a faulty catch, or you simply haven't closed it correctly. In an ideal world these mistakes would not happen but we are working in a far from ideal world. You may be on a boat or remote destination where the facilities are far from perfect. So many factors can lessen your concentration, such as tiredness, cold, too much sun, seasickness, or maybe you were just chatting or distracted while closing the camera up – and as a result you've just overlooked a very simple and basic step.

Check for leaks before entering the water

4. When you've dunked your housing and checked for leaks one final check – make sure that the camera will turn on and off and all functions are operational. Just as it's easy to overlook something when closing up the housing, it's just as easy to forget something as simple as turning the camera on or attaching a remote cable – and once you're in the water it's too late. Many a dive has been wasted and many a shot been lost through overlooking these simple basics!

5. Make sure everything is attached correctly, particularly detachable parts such as filters. It is at the beginning of a dive when you have just entered the water and are getting all equipment sorted before descending that things can drop off and sink down or float away never to be found again.

6. Never jump into the water holding your camera. The impact could easily damage a seal or some other part of the mechanism.

7. Don't assume that the boat crew or your fellow divers will know how to handle your equipment, how to hand it down to you after you enter the water or how to take it from you when you are trying to get back in the boat after the dive. Explain to them how to hold it – what to grip and what not to grip – otherwise you may find someone lifting the unit by a part that is not meant to take the weight. If this happens it is your fault rather than theirs.

Explain how you want the camera handed to you

8. As soon as your camera is handed to you in the water, go through your leak checks. Firstly check all seals, connections, controls and lenses to make certain that there are no bubbles emerging. Almost all housings have a leak warning light so also check that, and repeat all these checks during your descent. A leak that may not be apparent at the surface will increase in flow as the pressure increases with descent, and a simple breach of an O-ring that may not be apparent at the surface could have developed into a steady trickle by 20m. If you spot a problem early enough you will still have a good chance of salvaging the situation.

9. You jump in the water and discover you have forgotten to turn on the camera inside the housing. There is an overwhelming temptation to get out again and open up the housing — don't! You are already dripping wet, so is the housing, and the boat is not the ideal place to open up the housing in any event. Far better one dive without the camera than risking water getting in. Nor should you think that as you are wet you can get someone still on board to do what you need on your instructions. It is almost always going to end in tears!

10 Never leave a housing or camera in direct sunlight. Not only is the heat potentially damaging, but lenses and eyepieces serve as magnifying glasses, and you only have to remember playing with a magnifying glass to direct the sun onto paper when you were a kid to realise the damage that can cause.

! Get that buzz...

One of my most bizarre filming experiences came several days into an intensive diving trip in Indonesia. 30m down on the seabed alongside a wreck I was amazed to see a mosquito coming in and out of shot! At first I thought I was hallucinating, before enlightenment slowly dawned. The mosquito had got into the housing while I was changing tapes, and was now enjoying the delights of a 30m wreck dive. Needless to say, the footage from that dive, though thoroughly entertaining, was unusable.

🔖 Laundry baskets!

Whether on a liveaboard or land based, the most valuable piece of equipment you can invest in is a plastic laundry basket! Many resorts and boats have their own variation on this theme – a storage system for camera equipment in which to transport cameras from the shore onto the boat, to keep them in during the boat journey, and to return them to immediately after the dive. The basket will protect the camera from knocks and contact with other equipment, is easy for you and the crew to carry and if it does slide around the deck at all the plastic and not the housing absorb the impact. Your boat may have an equally satisfactory system, but it is surprising how many don't, in which case buy or borrow one at your destination. It's cost will be minimal so it is a disposable item that you can leave behind at the end of the trip.

Taking your time

Observe your subject. The longer you spend with just one creature the more you see the more you learn about them and the better the story is that you have to tell.

I will often spend ten minutes or more with just one simple subject before I am satisfied that I have enough useable footage and I can safely move on.

Sometimes I'll use up a whole tank of air in one place on one subject before I'm satisfied that I've got the shots I need – and I have been known to get a second tank and go back again!

The two sequences on the opposite page were the result of just this.

Length of shots

The techniques of still and video work underwater differ greatly, and without getting into the never to be resolved argument of which is easier, the principal problem that the videographer has to overcome that do not affect a stills photographer is the length of time needed to take a shot.

For stills, once a shot is set up, one flash and the image is captured; not so for us. To be of any use at all a video shot needs to be a minimum of six seconds in length – and preferably longer. Watch any documentary on television and count off the length of individual shots and you will see this rule of thumb in operation. While occasionally shorter shots can be edited together in a rapid-fire sequence, for a film to flow smoothly and to give people time to appreciate the shot six seconds is the average.

Although as a general rule they are to be used sparingly, longer shots are often justified if you have interesting behaviour or even just a fish swimming through your frame. But otherwise think of six to eight seconds as being the average length of a

useable shot. Then add a second each end to give a bit of leeway in the edit, and you are looking at a shot perfectly lit, framed, and without camera movement of around ten seconds to be useable. This is the most common mistake with beginners. They think simply in terms of 'getting, the shot' which usually entails lots of wobbling around until the subject appears for a moment perfectly in frame. Believing they have 'got' the shot they move onto the next subject. I call this the 'stills mentality' – get a shot and move on.

Only when you start editing – and I cannot stress too often how integral a part of underwater film-making editing actually is – will you start to realise how wrong this technique is. Not only do you want steady shots of your subject of a useable length, but you need a variety of shots. You are not putting together a slide show of single shots of different creatures – you are a storyteller, your camera is your storytelling tool, and the images must tell your story.

Sequence 1: a surprise feeding

On a night dive, Fionn was focusing on this octopus in an old tin can. He didn't even notice the antenna of the shrimp passing the bottom of the frame, but the octopus did! By taking time to get the shot of the octopus he ended up with far more – a completely unexpected feeding sequence!

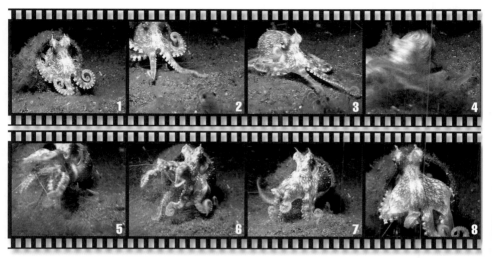

Frame 1: Octopus in can. Frame 2: shrimp enters the frame. Frames 3–5 : Octopus emerges from can and snatches shrimp. Frames 6-8: Octopus returns to can to eat his prey.

Sequence 2: jawfish mating

I'd been looking for a jawfish shot so when I found this one actively cleaning its burrow I settled down to spend some time getting all the shots I might need – wide-angles, close-up's, behaviour shots. But what happened next was totally unexpected. A female swam into shot and began laying her eggs in the male's mouth. Unique footage that I would have missed had I not taken my time with my subject.

Frame 1: Jawfish. Frame 2: A female swims past. Frames 3–4 : Male jawfish leaves burrow to approach female Frame 5: Male Jawfish 'swallows' female Frames 6–7: Female lays eggs in male's mouth. Frame 8: Female leaves.

Steady shots

To be useable a shot must be steady. Most cameras have a steady shot function but this is not enough – you have to contend with current, surge, and be able to hold a camera totally steady and perhaps also follow a moving sea creature for many seconds while struggling with all these factors while never forgetting the basic rules of diving. Just try holding a video camera steady for ten seconds at home and then imagine trying to do it 20m underwater on a wall in surge while trying to maintain buoyancy and position.

You will learn totally new diving skills and hone your buoyancy control to the finest of arts To get a shot the stills photographer can hover in the most awkward of positions – only for the split second of the shot do they need to be stationary. You, by contrast, will need to develop the art of remaining stable for lengthy periods without flattening all the coral and everything else within your vicinity and without kicking up a snowstorm of sand or silt that would inevitably wreck your shot

Some creatures are shy and react to lights and immediately take flight or hide. The stills photographer will have got his shot by the time the creature reacts – you do not enjoy this luxury and so will have to develop immense patience as you stalk your subject. Mandarinfish are a typical example – a favourite image in dive magazines because of their wonderful colouration and features, yet little good video footage of mandarinfish has been shot for this very reason.

Mandarinfish

Keep your shots steady!

After 3 days sitting on the jury of a video contest I was feeling decidedly seasick! In so many of the films the camera was moving about so much that all the jury were feeling nauseous trying to watch them! Not keeping the camera steady is the biggest single common mistake that beginners make.

Correct your mistakes

One advantage of video is the bonus of immediate playback through a television screen or camera monitor immediately after the dive. Some housings actually allow you this facility while you are still underwater, though use this sparingly as rewinding and reviewing footage will quickly drain the camera battery.

However when back on the surface, take advantage of this ability to review your footage in order to correct mistakes. The lighting may not be quite right; there may be a mark on the lens that you didn't notice through the smaller viewfinder that becomes apparent on the bigger screen. Learn by your mistakes.

Ask the questions – did I get the shots I wanted? If so, could I have done it differently – different angle, movement, lighting? And if not, then try and do better on the next dive!

Ethics -how far will you go to get a shot

Tales abound of how other film-makers have obtained spectacular footage. Where do you draw the line between gently and carefully manipulating a creature to a different position to enhance your shot and ruthlessly getting the shot at no matter what cost to the creature or its habitat? Gently teasing an octopus out of a burrow to which it will be able to safely return is a million miles from destroying its habitat to force it into the open so you can get the image you want. My personal rule is to draw the line at any conduct that will harm the creature or its environment.

Be aware of your impact on your surroundings. While all looks beautiful and at peace ahead of you through the viewfinder, behind your fins you may be smashing the corals, or churning up the sea bed as you kick to keep yourself steady. No shot can justify destroying the environment you have come to film.

Diving considerations

Remember that when diving with a camera there will be more drag and you are carrying extra weight, so always keep a close eye on air consumption. Develop the best technique for swimming with the camera to minimise drag, particularly in strong currents, by keeping the housing as close to your body as you can. Don't get so engrossed in filming that you don't have sufficient air to surface safely and carry out any deco stops. Keep a check on your position relative to the boat and the shore. It is too easy to spend your bottom time so focused on filming that you have no idea where you are and stray dangerously far from safety.

Above all, remember all the rules of diving. You are first and foremost a diver and second a cameraman.

Air consumption is a major consideration for underwater film-makers

With or without a buddy?

Having just told you to remember all the rules of diving, it is a fact of life that many photographers and video cameramen often dive alone. It may take a long time – sometimes a whole dive, working with just one subject until achieving that perfect shot, the octopus leaving it's burrow or of the cleaner shrimp in the mouth of the moray. Few dive buddies have the patience to remain with you while you work on getting your shot. So to dive alone is a decision that only you can make. But whatever you decide it is a decision that you must make before and not during the dive, and one that you must discuss with your buddy, with any other divers and with the boat crew. There is no mid-way position and your decision must be clear and known to all.

Be prepared

Always enter the water with a fresh battery in the camera and plenty of tape. The dive when you decide to go in and finish off a tape is sure to be the dive when you run out. Tape is cheap so if in doubt use a fresh one. If your tape is part used and you have some good footage from a previous dive already on it then again use a new tape - don't risk ruining or losing what you have already achieved.

And although this chapter is about planning your shoot – plan for the unexpected. Always try and save a minute or two at the end of the tape for when you are ascending. It always seems to be when you've totally finished the tape that a school of dolphins passes during your safety stop!

Etiquette

If you are not going to become the most hated diver in the group you must observe the film-makers etiquette.

If the subject is just passing by or if there's action happening such as feeding or mating, the rule is first come, first served. If someone else has found the action, give them a reasonable time to get their shot without interfering, - though if they end up hogging the action a gentle tap on the shoulder may remind them that others would also like a chance to capture an image. If you don't follow this rule then the likelihood is that no-one will get shots or footage worth having, as in the frenzy of bubbles, lights, flashing strobes and stirred up sand it's likely that the creatures will be totally spooked and either stop what they were doing or make a very speedy exit.

If others are waiting then don't be a critter hog – after a reasonable length of time let others have a go, and the chances are that if the situation is reversed and they find the action first they will do the same for you. Don't be afraid to discuss this etiquette with others you are diving with and try and agree some ground rules. Also don't be shy about explaining to stills photographers that if they take shots while you are filming, the flash of their strobe will ruin your whole sequence.

However, if the subject is sedentary like the frogfish then hold back, let the stills photographers have their turn as they will get their shots and move on. You will then have the luxury of your subject for as long as you want without someone breathing impatiently over your shoulder. Settle down, get comfortable, get your breathing slow and regular, let the particles in the water settle, and take some great shots. And when you've finished shooting, leave causing as little disturbance as you can as someone else may want to film the same creature without having to wait for your snowstorm of sand to settle.

Don't be a 'critter-hog'. get your shot and move on

Here are some mistakes that I've made and expensive lessons that I've learned!

! Partial flood in Palau

In Palau, a combination of many hours underwater every day, the hot tropical sun, and lunch on the beach where we were taking our midday break had made me drowsy. The water was still and clear and the shallow corals just off the beach were just too inviting. Snorkelling would not only cool me down and wake me up, but I should be able to get some half and half shots. I knew my battery was low, so replaced it and waded in.

It was only after about 20 minutes that I realised the droplets of water were not on the outside of the housing but inside. Instead of finding a sensible place to open the housing to change

batteries I'd done it sitting on the beach and in my semi-sun struck drowsiness I'd not checked the O-ring before closing up the housing – after all, I was only going snorkelling! Grains of sand had got on the O-ring and allowed a slow trickle of water into the housing. Although not totally flooded, the water that had got in was enough to not only ruin the camera, but had also penetrated the electrics of the housing, and there was no way that on a beach on a deserted island nor on a basic dayboat that I could either try fresh water or dry out camera and housing. Both were ruined.

! Camera loss in Cayman

I drowned my first camera on my first real underwater filming trip. I was on Grand Cayman and had rented a small self-drive boat for the duration of my stay. That way I could dive where I wanted when I wanted and for as long as I wanted.

I'd decided to do a night dive on a wreck that was not normally dived at night and the word had got around - friends and off duty dive guides also wanted to come and I ended up as boatman, organiser and divemaster as well as cameraman. People were missing equipment, others late, the boat needed loading. By the time I'd sorted everyone else's problems, I just had time to quickly check my camera and get on board to motor out to find the site before it got

completely dark.

Within seconds of rolling off the boat my camera felt unusually heavy, but I was so distracted and tired that it didn't register that something was wrong until I was on the sea bed at 20m, by which time the housing was full of water. Only then did I remember that during the afternoon I'd removed and cleaned O-rings; preoccupied with everyone else's problems and with organising the dive I'd not checked my own equipment properly and had forgotten to replace an O-ring. The others had a spectacular dive – mine was aborted and a camera totally ruined, although on this occasion the housing, which was a mechanical one, survived to be used for the rest of the trip.

Lessons learned

1. Do a pre-dive check list. Establish a personal routine and make rules for yourself. Disasters are generally easy to avoid and usually come about in situations where you are distracted from your usual procedure and end up breaking your rules and routine.

2. Always religiously follow your pre-dive check list procedure before getting in the water

3 Never work on your camera in tricky surroundings such as on a beach or in an environment such as on a boat where there is the risk of water getting in.

4. Focus on your own equipment and diving – leave everything else to the others

Try and avoid distractions when getting ready

You can't open the housing underwater nor should you on a small boat or on the beach, so before and after every dive you should have a check list of jobs, a routine that you religiously follow.

Before every dive

1. Make sure that all lenses and ports are spotlessly clean inside and out. A mark, smear or speck that may not be noticeable through the viewfinder will show up clearly as a blemish on a larger screen and can stay there wrecking footage from many dives if you only clean the lens sporadically.
2. Carry out O-ring maintenance or checks.
3. Check that the camera is securely fixed in the housing and all cables attached.
4. Ensure that the camera is switched on and any settings that need to be set before the housing is closed are correctly set.
5. Close the housing, ensuring that no cables, hairs or any other objects are trapped.
6. Whenever possible immerse the housing in fresh water and look carefully for air bubbles that might indicate a possible leak. If this is not possible, either wade into the water or at the start of the dive immerse the housing to a depth of at least a metre and check for tell-tale bubbles.

Bubble check

There is always some container available that can be filled with fresh water to enable you to check that your housing is watertight before every dive, and if not then insist that the resort or dive boat provides one! A rinse tank, large bucket, a fish box, anything that is large enough and will hold water will do. If all else fails gently lower the housing into the water before you get in and watch for telltale bubbles.

After every dive

1. Rinse the housing thoroughly in fresh water. Give the buttons and controls particular attention to prevent salt deposits building up.
2. Before opening the housing, ensure that it is thoroughly dry and that you are also thoroughly dry.
3. When opening the housing hold the part containing the camera pointing upwards so any residual water on the outside will not get into the housing. Always have a towel available and mop up every single drop of water.

4. Never leave the housing open in a place with high humidity and moisture.
5. If the housing is sealed up in a place with high humidity, condensation may occur on the inside of the glass port when the housing is in the water. Similarly, if camera and/or housing have been kept in an air conditioned environment moisture may form on them on leaving that environment, which will result in condensation. Always ensure that both camera and housing are absolutely dry before sealing them up - a hair drier is a great accessory to ensure that every bit of moisture is removed.
6. When storing the housing for any period of time, clean it externally in warm, fresh water to ensure that every bit of salt is removed, and also remove clean and grease all screws, nuts and bolts. Place silica gel bags inside to draw any moisture from the air inside the housing. These can be bought in photography stores. Indeed, they can be taped inside the housing even when in use as long as they do not interfere with the operation of the controls to help keep the interior dry and moisture free. You should follow a similar maintenance programme with lights and mounting brackets. In addition to thorough washing, unscrew all nuts and bolts and lubricate/grease them so that they do not seize up during storage.

Head games

Repeated use of the camera to play back footage will increase wear on the heads and shorten the life of the camera. Depending on the amount of filming and playback that you plan to do it can be worthwhile to invest in a separate tape player which will prolong the useful life of the camera by using it only for its main function - filming!

When I returned a relatively new video camera to the manufacturer because it had developed a fault I was told that I would have to pay for the heads to be replaced as the camera had been used far more than they would expect. That one repair alone cost me more than buying a player for the camera tapes.

Try to avoid overusing the playback facility of your camera as to do so can greatly reduce the lifespan of the camera. Purchasing a player for your tapes, either with its own monitor or simply one that can be plugged into any compatible screen, will greatly extend the useful life of the camera.

Air con risk

Never open and close a housing in an air conditioned environment, as this will invariably result in condensation forming on the inside of the port of the housing during the dive, fogging visibility and making footage from the dive unusable

Care of tapes

Everything you have spent and done has been to produce the shots on the camera tapes, so these are very valuable and also need care. Ensure all are tabbed to prevent accidental re-use and erasure of footage. Store them in a dry, cool place away from direct sunlight and from any heat source

Silica gel

Silica gel packs can be bought in photography shops. Taped inside the housing they can help to keep the interior dry and moisture free

You can buy silica gel in packs, and it is always worth attaching a couple inside the housing where they will not interfere with the operation of the camera in order to remove any moisture that may be in the housing. Another option is to make your own.

1. Cut the toe off a ladies stocking
2. Fill it with silica gel granules
3. Knot it and tie in a convenient place in the housing.

The transparency of the nylon lets you check when the colour of the granules changes indicating that they have absorbed moisture and need replacing.

Avoid cabbage soup!

We were moored off Assumption Island in the south of the Seychelles archipelago and it was an open deck day – a wide bay with no current for us to dive for as long and as often as we wished. Before lunch I had found a fascinating cleaning station on a small coral head a few hundred metres from the dive ship, where cleaner wrasse were swimming in and out of the mouths and gills of large sweetlips. Two bowls of the cook Netta's finest Israeli cabbage soup and I was back in the water, inching closer to the cleaning action, when the cabbage soup took its laxative effect, and I had to go – and soon!

There was no chance of me making it back to the ship in time but with no other divers anywhere near I decided to try a manoeuvre not included in any training manual. First laying down the camera safely, I removed the BC keeping the regulator in place, then weight belt over the knees, stripped the wetsuit down – and relief – until I felt a repeated nipping sensation on my exposed posterior and turning saw that my actions had started a feeding frenzy. Like a Caribbean fish feed, dozens of yellowtails, small snapper and wrasse had homed in on the unexpected feast, giving the term 'bottom feeding fish' a new meaning!

There is a serious lesson to be learnt – what you eat and drink can have a direct and unexpected effect on your dive and so on your ability to collect footage.

Planning your shoot

Whether you are an underwater stills photographer who has moved into video, a videographer who has moved into diving, or a diver who is new to filming, you must put aside all preconceptions. To film successfully underwater you have to think differently – think video – think story. What is the story you are going to tell and how are you going to capture it with your camera? What do you want to say and what sequence and shots will visually convey it?

Unlike a scripted land based film shoot, you have no control over what you will see during your dive, as most ocean creatures are unpredictable, however, you will usually have a general idea of what you will be seeing. It may be a wreck dive, a location where shark are often seen, or just a general reef dive. Wherever the dive, you should always have a good idea of what you hope to film and how you will use the shots when you come to edit. Your film will tell a story, so make sure that you have an idea of the shots you will need to put that story together.

Telling a story

Even if filming something simple such as coral, follow the same rules – at the very least take wide-angle shots that set the scene, mid-range shots to show the particular coral, and close-ups of the individual polyps. This simple rule of wide, medium and close-up is the very minimum number of shots of a useable length that you should be taking.

But don't just do the minimum! Be creative – think of other angles, other ideas – think of the story you want to tell!

Even if you are simply trying to show the variety of colourful fish on the reef, vary your shots, otherwise your film will look more like an animated fish identification book than a film telling a story. Film the fish facing in different directions, mix in some closer shots with wider shots, take advantage of the fact that you are recording moving images and capture movement in your shots – for example a fish coming into frame, or as your final shot have a fish leaving frame and 'wiping' the frame clean with its tail.

When filming underwater think of the story you want to tell and take the shots that will do just that. You have in your hands the greatest story telling tool and means of entertainment that you could hope for – use it as that, not simply as a different sort of stills camera!

Planning your shoot is very easy to ignore – the argument that you have no control over what comes along underwater and therefore can make no plans can be a persuasive one. However a dive with a camera is not generally as uncertain as many would argue, and the better prepared you are the better the footage will be.

Try different angles and use props or divers to give a sense of scale

Promotional film for the dive boat FeBrina

This sequence did not happen by chance – to put together what is just a 15 second segment of a promotional film for the dive boat FeBrina took a lot of planning. Firstly we had to find the dolphins on a flat calm day.

Shots 1 and 2 were taken from the inflatable running alongside the ship as she passed through the school.

Shot 3 was taken from the bow of FeBrina looking down onto the dolphins riding the bow wave.

Shot 4 was taken by leaning off the bow of the inflatable and holding the housing in the water, giving the impression that we were actually swimming with the school.

Finally to get **shots 5 and 6** Fionn got in the water, we then drove the ship with the dolphins riding the bow wave towards him so he could get the underwater shots of the ship and dolphins. A lot of planning and work with the captain and crew to get a variety of shots that when edited together create an impressive sequence.

Think before you get wet

What are you trying to achieve on this dive? Are you simply going to collect some general footage, or maybe tell the story of the dive?

Before entering the water you will know the type of dive site and the likely subjects you will be filming. Is it a wreck dive where you will be filming mainly wide-angle shots? Or a muck dive where you will be filming macro subjects. How your camera is set up and which lenses filters and dioptres you will be using must be decided before getting into the water.

Think about the physical conditions in which you will be filming and use your knowledge of both your subject and the dive site to get the most you can from the dive. Visibility will often be poorer on an outgoing tide than an incoming tide. When will the light be at its best? What time of day will the creatures you want to film be active?

Water is never crystal clear. It always contains particles and plankton, and these affect filming in a number of ways. The denser the material in the water the less light penetrates, and the less visibility there is. The effect of using lights in water dense with plankton or sediment is similar to driving in fog with headlights on full beam, and the lights reflecting off the particles create scatter.

This can be doubly frustrating as some of the largest and most emotive film subjects are plankton feeders and will be found where the plankton is the thickest and therefore where the visibility is lowest. That is why so little good footage exists of basking shark that visit the Atlantic coasts of northern Europe each summer, their arrival coinciding with the spring plankton bloom.

You have no control over plankton, but there are ways to minimise the occurrence of sediment and suspensions in the water. If filming near the coast, incoming tide is almost always preferable to a falling tide that will carry with it debris and mud from the shore. An incoming tide is generally bringing fresh water flowing in from the ocean, not dragging dirty water from the land.

Avoid river mouths and estuaries unless that is the only place to find your subject – rivers carry suspended material that they have collected on their journey. Avoid filming close to land after heavy rain – the run-off from the land will cloud the water and reduce visibility. These are all factors that should be considered when selecting your dive site.

An area totally within your own control is the amount of sand and silt you kick up! There is a fine line to tread. I always advise that you should carry slightly more weight if you may wish to settle on the bottom to film steadily, so buoyancy control becomes even more essential. Minimise the disturbance you cause when settling down to film, and be especially aware of your fin movements. Whenever possible situate yourself down current of your subject so debris stirred up will be washed away from you and your subject. Sand and silt will cause reflection of light and make it appear that you have been filming in an underwater snowstorm!

Filming Basking sharks is never easy due to plankton blooms

Watch where you place your fins

📋 Tip Put it on the slate

While pre-planning and a detailed briefing is essential, always carry a divers slate so you can communicate extra instructions underwater. It's also always worth having some agreed signals that everyone understands – otherwise how do you explain to someone underwater that you want them to position themselves behind this particular anemone and look at it while you film them?

The storyboard

The storyboard is the device used by all film-makers including major Hollywood producers. It need not be a work of art, as long as it is sufficient for you to plan the shoot and ensure that you get all the footage that you will need.

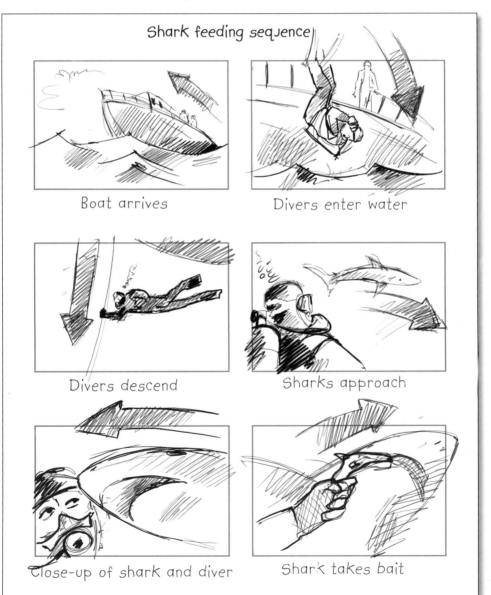

Shark feeding sequence

Boat arrives

Divers enter water

Divers descend

Sharks approach

Close-up of shark and diver

Shark takes bait

Seahorse at night

6. Lighting

Proper use of lights can make or break a shot. Remember the golden rule – look at what you are actually shooting. Never does this apply more than when using lights. Proper use of lights such as positioning, distance from subject, angle and strength of light very often get overlooked, the film maker simply turning on the lights and pressing 'Record'. The resulting mistakes can be over exposure, glare, insufficient light, shadow and scatter, which may ruin what would otherwise have been a good shot. All of these mistakes are avoidable if you look at the shot analytically before taking it

Lights are necessary because unlike air, water is not transparent, and the deeper you go the more the sun's light is filtered out, so although within the first few metres there is sufficient sunlight to film successfully without lights, the deeper you go the more light is lost. Also, as it travels through the water column the colours in sunlight are absorbed, warmer colours such as reds being the first to be lost, so by 20 metres everything appears to have a blue colour in tropical waters and green in colder waters. I have been in a submersible to 300 metres underwater, and there everything appeared dull grey. Colour correction filters can help to restore the natural colours of the spectrum that have been lost with depth, but lights can also achieve this and can add illumination in places where it would otherwise be impossible to film due to the lack of natural light such as in caves and crevices, in shipwrecks, at night, or simply on overcast and dull days

Why do we need video lights?

The sun's rays cannot travel through water in the same way as they do through air. Air is transparent; water is not. Water is far denser than air so as rays of light travel through water they encounter both molecules of water and also sediment, particles and living plankton that are suspended in the water. These all block and deflect light with the result that the longer the water column through which light has to travel – in other words the deeper you are – the less the light.

Furthermore, different elements of the light spectrum are absorbed at differing rates – remember the Colour Absorption chart on page 30.

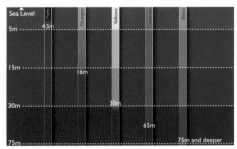

It tends to be the warmer colours – the reds and the yellows - that are filtered out first, leaving the colder colours, which is why everything underwater tends to appear blue and eventually if you go very deep grey.

Lights help to restore the lost colours of the spectrum by providing an artificial light source that is close to the subject. While colour correction filters can go some way to helping to restore a natural colour balance, the deeper you go, the duller the day, the murkier the water, or when filming in a wreck or cave or at night, then the less their effectiveness.

Generally only in the shallowest and clearest of water in good sunshine will you be able to film successfully without lights. So it is essential that you get familiar with use of lights and also experiment with the various camera settings to obtain the optimum results. This is where understanding the white balance control of your camera is critical.

White balance

While not fully understood by many videographers even on dry land, white balance is probably one of the most crucial elements of successful video. The technical definition of white balance is the means by which the camera adjusts to varying lighting conditions such as outdoor sunlight or indoor artificial light. There is usually a selection of settings on a camera which will allow you to preselect either of these settings or an automatic setting that will leave the decision to the camera.

In simpler terms white balance is a way of telling the camera what white looks like in any particular light so that it then knows what other colours should look like by comparison.

On land the common practice of professional cameramen is to manually white balance, as often the pre-set alternatives of sunlight or artificial light settings are just an average level. Find something white such as a piece of paper or card and following the instructions for your particular camera focus on that white item and manually

white balance. You will see the colour balance change to adapt to the specific lighting conditions in which you are shooting.

Underwater pure white objects are not as easy to come by as on land, yet white balancing is equally important if not more so as the light conditions are never as good as on the surface. So how to white balance?

My tip is that you paint one or both of your fins white, and white balance by focusing on these before every shot. If you will be using lights for the shot then turn them on before white balancing.

You should white balance regularly, if not before every shot, then certainly every time you change position or subject.

Over Exposure

This term means over-lighting the subject. Lights on full glare close to the subject will result in an unusable shot; the delicate colours that are possessed by most underwater creatures are lost and a shiny, one- coloured creature remains. Look at the shot before filming.

If the subject is over lit, either turn down your lights until the lighting is complementary or, if you have no dimmer facility, the same effect can be achieved by increasing the distance between lights and creature either by bending the light arms further back or moving the whole housing. Another technique is to alter the angle of the lights so that they are not shining directly on the animal, point them slightly away from the subject and the result will be a reduction in the direct light, a reduction in glare, and a more subtle lighting.

Hot Spots

Over lighting can also be identified by 'hot spots' – the reflection of white light back from the subject. The solutions are the same – redirect the light or reduce it until the hot spot disappears.

If you use the camera's automatic functions to find exposure levels and white balance then these are your best options. If your housing allows you to override the cameras automatic functions then manually adjusting the camera exposure can also work – but be careful not to eliminate hot spots at the expense of dulling down the rest of the image.

Many cameras have a zebra function – if activated a pattern of diagonal stripes will be displayed on the viewfinder. These appear on any part of the image where there is excessive brightness or over exposure. These zebra stripes are a helpful addition to draw your attention to what you should be seeing with your own eyes if you are following our basic rule of seeing what you are looking at through the viewfinder. Adjusting the exposure, shutter speed, angle and proximity of lights should eliminate these hot spots.

Insufficient light

Insufficient light can ruin footage just as much as over-lighting – if the lights are too distant or too dim to adequately light the subject. Lights bring out the natural colours and add dimension to a flat portrait, and if lighting is too weak, the shot will not be strong. The solutions are the converse of those for over lighting and hot spots, namely increase the output of your lights if you can, move either the lights themselves or the whole housing closer, redirect the angle of the lights, and if using manual settings check and adjust the exposure control.

Without...   *and with lights*

Shadow

Shadow can spoil a shot in many ways. While occasionally it is a technique that you may wish to use to achieve effect, usually it is unintentional. The commonest fault is that the direction of the light throws a part of the subject into shadow, so check the angle of the lights and the direction in which they are pointing. Shadow can be a particular problem when using only one light and even more so when the light is fixed to the housing by a rigid rather that flexible arm to the housing. Two lights on flexible arms are always preferable. Remember to look at the image you are getting before shooting – if there are areas of shadow or only part of the subject is lit, adjust before recording.

Some light settings are almost inevitably going to create unwanted areas of shadow such as filming from directly above. Use whatever flexibility you have in your lighting system to your maximum advantage, don't be afraid to detach lights if it will create a better effect.

Experiment

Be imaginative in your use of lights. Despite having almost unlimited flexibility with lights, most people use a simple frontal assault on their subject. This can result in a flat light, areas of shadow, and a series of shots of very different subjects that look disappointingly similar because of an identical lighting approach.

Rigid arm lighting systems give little flexibility and are generally only suitable for wide-angle shots. For closer shots flexible arm systems are the better choice.

Don't be afraid of unscrewing lights from housings to use them for side or back lighting a shot where the opportunity arises. Use flexible arms to their full capability – they don't both have to be pointing at the subject from equal angles. Look through the viewfinder – is one side of the shot brighter than the other, is part of the shot in shadow? Be innovative – maybe use one of the arms to light your subject from below

Sometimes it is also worth not only looking through the housing, but over it, as you may then see far more clearly exactly where your lights are falling relative to your subject and so adjust them. However looking through the viewfinder is always the best – what you see there is what you will get.

Learn to recognise when a shot is just not going to work because you can't get the lighting right. In those situations it's best just to give up rather than waste battery life and tape!

Most of all, when you have learnt all the rules be prepared to break them! As I keep on repeating, look through your viewfinder to see exactly what the image you are getting looks like, and adjust lights and all other variables until you achieve the optimum image.

Correct lighting is essential to pick out the true colours and details of your subjects

The natural beauty of the underwater
world revealed by artificial lighting

Shrimp in bubble coral

7. Specific filming techniques

Never forget that with a video camera we are not collectors of a series of images that will become a video slide show; we are story tellers. We are not simply taking a series of portraits – we are recording movement and behaviour. So you must be innovative and get as great a variety of shots as possible – general wide angles, close-up shots, mid-range shots, things moving into and out of shot, tracking shots. Think carefully about setting up your shots to record behaviour and movement, not just simple portraits. Although there is always a place in a film for that good shot of a fish close up and full frame, vary your shots and think about movement, lighting, silhouettes, and composition.

General – wide, medium and close

There is a basic rule of thumb that instructors in videography have been using for years – that you should shoot your subject in three ways in order to have sufficient shots to edit together successfully. This is the rule of wide angle, medium range, and close-up. As a starting point there is nothing wrong with this rule because it teaches the basic idea that you must shoot a variety of shots to be able to edit a story. However the rule is only the starting point.

Frame 1: Wide   Frame 2: Medium   Frame 3: Close-up

Moving shots

Videographers have an added dimension in which to work - movement. With a stationary subject we can move the camera towards or away from it, or pan from one side to the other or up/down to the subject to create a far more interesting shot than a simple still shot. If the subject is itself moving then that very movement can be used to enhance our shot — subjects swimming into and out of frame or, for example, giving the viewer a view of a shipwreck by following a fish or diver along it.

When filming moving shots rather than filming from a fixed stationary position – tracking shots following a particular subject, or panning shots when we move the camera to reveal the subject – it is essential that all movements of the camera are smooth and slow. Any jerkiness will be massively magnified on a larger screen to the extent that the shot will be unwatchable. For surface filming expensive tripods with fluid heads can be bought to ensure smooth tracking and panning shots; underwater we are already in that fluid medium so have the advantage that our movements are already governed by the water itself, so smooth shots become far easier to achieve.

Letting subject 'clear frame', makes for a useful shot when editing

Setting up shots – silhouettes

Silhouettes are a favourite technique, and used properly can introduce an emotive feel to any film and can be ideal in the edit suite for ending a sequence and creating an atmosphere. Experiment with these shots and you will soon find the best angle is with the subject passing across the sunburst. If filming a silhouette try using light directed not at the subject but at the foreground, so creating not one but two points of interest in the shot – the subject in silhouette and also the foreground. The shot on page 65 is a good example of the effectiveness of this technique

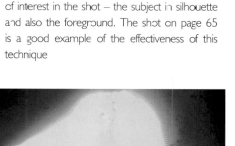

Setting up shots – composition

The composition of a shot is also the hallmark of a good cameraman. Positioning your subject centre frame in every shot will make for a very dull final production, so try different compositions of the same shot. Stills photographers use the rule of thirds – divide the screen into imaginary sectors horizontally and vertically and use these imaginary sectors as guides to positioning of the subject. Think of a noughts and crosses board and in your mind superimpose that grid pattern onto the image. Then position subjects not centrally in the frame, but in one of the imaginary boxes on the grid.

I. In the shot of the rope and sunburst (above), the initial inclination would be to have the sun in the centre of the frame with the rope running up to it. However by positioning the sun in the top left hand corner box of our imaginary grid, this produces a far more interesting shot.

2. Rather than focusing on the shark centre frame, leaving space in front of it enhances the feeling of movement.

3. The fish and diver forming the bottom third of the above image, with the middle third empty, and the sun in the top left hand corner of this portrait shot gives a far better feeling of scale and perspective than would have been achieved had diver and fish been centre frame.

4. The shot of the boat at sunset shows the application of this rule; rather than simply having sea and sky equal with the boat centre frame there is more sky than sea and the boat is offset from the centre of the shot. Instead of having the dividing line between sea and land or sea and sky neatly cutting a screen in half, a far better effect is achieved by a larger proportion of the screen being taken up by the feature on which you want the viewer to focus.

Choice of background

After selecting your subject, think about the background against which you are filming your subject. By carefully selecting your position you can make a shot far more interesting. An image of a fish with nothing behind it may be less interesting than a fish passing the bow of a wreck or through a rock arch.

Always be aware of natural light. If you have the sun behind you, the fish will be far better lit than if you are filming towards the sun, when the actual subject will be part silhouette. If a shot is backlit – if the light source is behind the subject – then depending on the strength of that light source the amount of detail on the subject will be reduced. So, unless it is your intention to create a silhouette effect, always try and keep the light source behind the camera. By simply adjusting the camera position relative to the light source you will notice through the viewfinder a radical difference in the quality of shot.

Filters

To overcome the loss of colours underwater it is necessary to use filters, lights, and sometimes both. Take a torch down on a dive and shine it on the reef or on fish and see the colours come alive. The torch is in fact simply replacing the natural light that has been absorbed by the water. Lights are discussed in chapter 6, but a few simple tips on the use of filters may help. The general rule, albeit with some exceptions, is if using lights then do not also use a filter. The lights should be sufficient to restore colour when used correctly, and if used in conjunction with a filter your film will have a hot, red glow to all the shots.

Never use the red filter in the first couple of metres of water, as your film will have an unnatural red hue to it. This is why it is essential to select a housing that allows you to choose during a dive whether or not to use the red filter. So if, for example, filming people getting into or out of boats, or subjects at the surface such as turtles or sea snakes taking air, or filming a shallow reef top, you will generally find it best to remove the red filter. On most housings checking through the viewfinder will show which looks the better.

Below about 2m a filter will be essential, certainly for wide-angle shots of divers, larger creatures, and general underwater scenes. And even a filter cannot compensate for colour loss through the water column, so remember the golden rule is the closer to the subject, the better the shot. Whether with or without a colour correction filter, the less water between your camera and your subject, the less colour absorption occurs. If you are anything more than two metres from your subject it will appear drab and blue washed, and the closer you get the better the camera will pick up the natural colours and the stronger the shot will be.

With no filter, the colours are washed out and lifeless

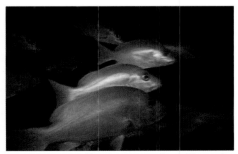

The incorrect use of a red filter makes the image un-natural

When to use and not to use autofocus

It may be stating the obvious, but a shot will be totally unusable if it is even slightly out of focus, or 'soft'. While it is easier to spot a soft shot on a larger screen, you should be able to recognise this through the viewfinder and by making manual focus adjustments be able to produce the sharpest image.

Auto-focus can be very useful if used as an aid to precise focus, but counter productive if over used.

A common fault with many beginners is to use auto-focus for all shots. There is a place for the use of auto-focus – but it is not for wide- angle moving shots. The slightest interference with the subject, such as a fish passing or even some debris in the water, can cause the camera to search for focus and the whole shot will be unusable. For moving shots always use manual focus, and for any shot more than 3 metres away set that focus to infinity, which is indicated by the mountain symbol on most cameras.

There are times when auto-focus can be a useful tool. When filming a stationary object the auto-focus function can be used to achieve sharp focus very quickly and will adjust to any change in distance between camera and subject. In such circumstances I personally will use the auto-focus as a guide and then switch to manual focus and make any further focus adjustments myself

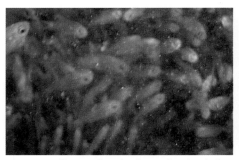

The auto-focus has focussed on the plankton

Manually focused on the fish

How to film fish

To film fish properly, you first need to observe and understand their behaviour. Rarely will a shot of a frightened fish's tail disappearing into the distance win you many awards or make for good viewing! Chasing fish is not how to film them. First let the fish get accustomed to your presence, settle down, regulate your breathing, and allow them to get back into their regular routine.

By doing this you will start to notice that many fish are territorial, and often follow a regular pattern of movement. This way, instead of a shot in which the fish is if full frame for the duration of the shot, by predicting the fish's movements you can produce a shot where it swims into frame, you follow its movements for a while and then let it swim out of frame; an interesting and professional shot that will make the job of editing the sequence far easier.

Avoid sudden movements, not only of your whole body but even when working the light and camera controls. Smooth, slow movements are far less likely to spook your subject than jerky sudden rapid movements.

When a school of fish is spotted there can be an almost overwhelming temptation to swim directly into the centre of the school. The result is scattering fish and a disappointing shot. Instead, try to swim on a gradually converging course. Think about it – why do fish school? For protection from larger predators. By swimming alongside them rather than through them you are far less likely to disturb them and so be able to get long flowing shots of their natural schooling behaviour.

A fish filmed from above will rarely make a good shot. This sort of shot is generally flat and uninteresting. Images filmed from the same level as the fish, or looking slightly up at it are generally far more successful. Experiment with different angles. Square on to the subject is not always the best shot; a slightly different angle of approach can make a shot far more interesting and appealing.

The Golden Rule

One of video's great advantages is that what you see through the viewfinder is what you get, so look through the viewfinder or monitor, and actually consider what you see there. Don't just think that as your subject looks good the resulting shot will look good. There can be a whole range of factors that ruin the shot, ranging from something on your lens to poor focus or lighting. Always use the visual display and pay attention to what it is telling you. I have actually seen both still and video photographers simply point their cameras in the general direction of the subject and shoot without ever looking through the viewfinder at what they are actually filming. Point and shoot simply does not work!

"Diving with pilchards!"

This is how a photographer friend of mine describes his techniques for getting the most out of an underwater creature in order to get his shots. By this he means taking dead fish underwater as a lure to attract subjects to the camera. This is how many of the great underwater shots have been obtained.

We only have a limited time we can spend underwater, and the chance of witnessing a fish catching its prey in that short window we have into their world is remote. So in order to maximise the chance of getting that classic shot, divers who have studied their subjects have learnt that taking the right bait with them on a dive is the best way of achieving the shot they are looking for.

Local knowledge is usually essential here and will come from dive guides and dive shop owners in the area, as they are the people who over time will have got to know the local creatures and how best to lure them into the camera lights. Some feeds are obvious such as shark feeds – most top photographer's shark shots will have been obtained in this way. The Cayman Islands stingrays are another photographic subject that have got used to being fed. There are also some less obvious and unlikely feeding subjects. A friend of

mine has been feeding conger eels on a wreck off the Cornish coast and entertains his divers with their antics. Shots of giant cuttlefish enveloping the camera lens have been obtained by attaching a piece of fish to the camera housing.

If taking fish underwater as bait, ensure that the specific fish forms part of the natural diet of your subject. An example of what not to do is divers who fed boiled eggs to napoleon wrasse in the Red Sea – many attribute the marked decline in numbers of these wrasse to the havoc that eggs caused to their digestive systems. Make sure also that if using frozen rather than fresh bait, the fish is fully de-frosted for the same reasons.

My own most bizarre experience of feeding fish to get a shot came in Indonesia. Having found a frogfish on an earlier dive, I explained to my local guide that I would have my camera running and focused on the fish and that he should try and herd any fish in the vicinity into the strike zone. After around 5 minutes tightly focused through the viewfinder I was amazed to see a nudibranch drop onto the head of the motionless frogfish and slowly spiral past its mouth. Looking up I saw the guide with a handful of nudibranchs that he intended 'feeding' to the frogfish!

Filming wrecks

Wrecks don't have to be ships and divers help give scale to the subject matter

When filming underwater, most of the creatures will be moving, and the film will capture that movement. Undersea wrecks however are stationary objects, and it is essential when filming them to ensure that the film does not become just a series of still shots of the wreck. Movement and interest can be achieved in a number of ways.

Firstly, move the camera. Pan up and down, or from side to side, so that the shot reveals different aspects of the wreck. Swim towards, over, and into the wreck filming as you go to give the viewer the very real feeling of exploring the wreck with you. Follow a diver as they explore the wreck. Then get shots to cut with those; for example if you first film someone swimming down into a hatch or through a doorway, get that person to do it again and this time film from inside so that they are now swimming in towards the camera. Employ similar techniques when leaving the wreck. Remember to film plenty cutaways, closer shots of the face and eyes of the diver. A shot following him in may not cut easily to the next shot filmed from inside. However if firstly you follow him in, then show a closer shot of his face as he looks around and only then cut to the shot from inside with the diver swimming towards the

camera you may find this is a smoother edit and also gives the viewer the feeling of being involved in the exploration of the wreck. Sometimes you may be fortunate enough to be able to follow a fish or one of the inhabitants of the wreck - this can again make an interesting variation on the theme.

If the water is clear enough, use of a model or fellow diver can also produce a very dramatic impression of size and scale.

To get good clear shots on and inside a wreck, your diving skills need to be honed to perfection. Wrecks are almost always silty places. Brushing against a doorway or wall can result in a cascade of rust and muck clouding the water. Even your bubbles can dislodge debris from the ceilings of a cabin or hatch. Once you start clouding the water in this way the quality of the shots will deteriorate dramatically. As you will invariably be using lights on any internal shots, these particles in the water will reflect back your lights - remember my earlier comparison to using car headlights in fog - and will further reduce the quality and saleability of the footage. For these reasons, pre-dive planning of a shoot on a wreck is of the highest priority so that you and your fellow divers or model know exactly what is expected of

Sometimes even poor conditions can create eerie atmospheres to a barren wreck

them. You will therefore probably need to do several dives on a wreck to achieve the optimum footage, treating the earlier dives as scouting missions to get to know the subject, work out the best angles and shots, and to brief your colleagues on these. Rarely will you be able to produce an impressive wreck sequence on just one dive.

Lighting a wreck is also of crucial importance. While for some subjects such as macro filming a narrow beam of light can be preferable, in wreck diving the widest angle of beam will give the best spread of even lighting. The light that comes from your model's torch can also be used to good effect as while your wide-angle beam will generally illuminate the scene, the narrow and more concentrated beam from their torch will heighten the impression of searching and exploration. A similar effect can be achieved on night dives.

Once you have scouted the wreck and decided on the best shots to take, consider setting up other lights inside the wreck or briefing other divers on

Natural forms against man-made offer dynamic visual opportunities

areas that you would like illuminated to create a better overall lighting effect.

No loose ends!

Make sure that any model or other diver who you will be filming is well kitted out. Trailing octopus regulators and overlong weight belts look terrible on film. If using rental equipment ensure that the markings cannot be seen. Insist on new clean tanks if not using your own – chipped and scratched tanks with peeling paint will ruin a shot

Filming sharks

Above: The sleek lines of a Reef shark
Film strip below: A Bull Shark on the prowl

To maximise the opportunity to get good close footage of shark it is generally necessary to travel to places where shark encounters can be virtually guaranteed. These will either be where there are natural aggregations or regular sightings of a specific species, or where shark feeds have been established providing less natural but still stimulating and productive encounters with every sort of shark from the common reef shark to caged experiences with Great Whites.

I have absolutely no problem with well organised shark feeds. I don't believe that occasionally giving a free feed to a species that has been around for millions of years will change their behaviour pattern, and even if it did I believe that the positive benefits derived from these feeds substantially outweigh the effect on a few shark getting used to a free meal.

Shark encounters have served to de-demonise the shark, as ever more divers can admire these magnificent creatures at close quarters. The more people are educated about shark the more chance there is of public pressure building to prevent the extinction of many shark species and to outlaw the horrifically primitive shark finning industry. In many areas it is only the shark feeds and the revenue that these generate for the local economy that saves local populations of shark from being fished out. I would much prefer to see a marginal behavioural change in a shark recognising a free food hand-out than the terminal change of that shark on a fishmonger's slab, it's fins having been hacked off while it is still alive.

The trick of using shark feeds to best advantage is not to film the feed! Much of the shark footage you see on television has been shot at shark feeding

Film strip: The lightning reactions of a feeding Angel Shark – from being completely hidden in the sand to swallowing whole a passing fish.

This page: Top: Wobbegong. Above: Basking shark.

locations, but conceals this fact by the camera filming not the other divers and the action, but away from the feed, filming the shark coming and going without human interaction.

The Bahamas have pioneered the shark feeding industry and are a good place to get footage of Carribbean reef shark and other local species. Dive boats and resorts in many other destinations run their own local shark feeding encounters. However the truly great encounters are the totally natural ones, where aggregations of shark are attracted to a sea mount such as occurs with schooling hammerheads at Malpelo and Cocos Island, or where reef passages attract massive numbers of shark as occurs at Rangiroa and other Pacific lagoons. The still unexplained bull shark encounter at Walker's Cay, Bahamas is unforgettable. Other

locations give relatively guaranteed encounters with some of the greatest ocean roamers. The south-west coast of the UK in early summer always produces stunning basking shark encounters, and locations such as Seychelles at the right time of year are the place to film the ocean's greatest fish, the whale shark.

There is only one hint about filming shark – don't chase them. Despite their popular image, most shark are shy and will be easily spooked by a diver rushing towards them pumping out streams of noisy bubbles. Stay still and the shark's curiosity will bring it in closer as it checks you out.

And if you want your children to have the chance of the same thrill of encountering shark in the open ocean rather than in an aquarium, join the Shark Trust! (www.sharktrust.org)

Using models

Are you looking to achieve a special shot that will need the co-operation of some of the other divers – a silhouette shot or perhaps a diver looking at or interacting with a sea creature? If so, this needs to be planned in advance, as it is not easy to convey your detailed requirements once under water.

Many husband and wife dive teams know each other so well that they work as a team underwater with the model knowing exactly where and how to position themselves in relation to the camera, but this easy co-operation takes a long time to perfect. The more information that you give to your model and to any other divers who may be in shot, the more they will know what to do and what not to do, and the better the chance of a successful shoot.

For example, if you intend pointing the camera at other divers, let them know and tell them how to react. Do you want them to ignore the camera? Or look at it and swim towards it? Or wave at it?

If you don't tell them how to behave in advance, they will not be sure and you will not achieve the shot you are looking for. If you want them to simply ignore you and behave normally then stress this to them in advance. Should you want them to do something special then brief them fully. If you want to get shots of the other divers entering the water then explain this to them. Tell them how long you will need to get down and set up to film before they jump in, any signal you will give that you are ready, and where you want them to swim when they enter the water.

Explaining the shots you are trying to achieve becomes even more important when working in confined spaces such as a cave or a wreck. If your buddies don't know what you want then you can be sure that the footage you get will be a mess.

Brief them clearly, for example – *'I'll follow you into the cave; once inside point your torch around as if you are exploring the cave. When I turn my lights off wait till I get behind you and turn my lights on,*

then swim slowly out of the cave and I'll be following you out.' Clear directions that will ensure you get the sequence you are looking for.

Think of what you want to be able to achieve when you get home and edit the footage. The more experience you have of editing, the more you will start to realise the sort of shots you will need to tell the story. Continuing with the cave example, so far all you have is shots following the diver. To produce a professional edit, you may want to be able to cut the shot of the diver leaving the cave to a wide-angle shot of the diver emerging from the cave and swimming back to the anchor line. You obviously can't be in two places at once but will need both shots for editing the sequence. So plan ahead, think what shots you will want when you get back home to edit the film, and then brief the team. It can be worth preparing a list of 'shots to get' before the dive so that nothing gets overlooked.

No fluorescent colours!

On film fluorescent suits, weight belts and accessories leap out at the eye to the detriment of the rest of the image. After all, this is what they are designed to do, and their impact is even greater when contrasted to the more subtle colours of the underwater world. Learn a lesson from the masters; remember the Cousteau films when all the divers wore silver suits? They not only looked cool but did not have the impact that fluorescent colours do.

Pygmy Seahorse

8. Advanced techniques

Once you have mastered general wide angle filming it's time to move on to some specialised techniques. Macro photography has been popular with stills photographers for some time now, the filming of tiny sea creatures and close detail such as eyes, mouths and body texture of larger ones. Equally stunning macro images can be obtained on video. I'm also including a section on half and half filming, sometimes termed 'over and under', which is the technique of filming at the water surface and including both topside and underwater images in one frame. Half and half sequences can greatly enhance a film. Finally I've devoted a whole section to filming at night. I'm not the world's keenest night diver, as in many places there just seems to be less to see at night than by day. However in some places night diving can be a stunning revelation as the creatures of the day disappear and a whole new cast of strange characters emerges to feed and forage, and filming these requires specific skills.

Macro filming

Macro filming is an art form in itself. Modern cameras are capable of some amazing results and the key to successful macro photography can be purchased very cheaply from almost any camera store – dioptres, also known as close-up filters.

Dioptres

This is a lesson I learnt at the Antibes Film Festival when a film shot on the same subjects and using the same camera and housing as mine quite rightly won our category. Until I learned that the cameraman was using dioptres I couldn't understand how just about every shot was closer, larger, and better than mine.

A dioptre is a screw on lens that attaches directly to the lens of the camera. Though primarily thought of as a tool for still photographers these work equally well for video. Most video cameras accept a screw on filter onto the camera lens and a range of dioptres are the essential tool for the macro videographer. Dioptres can be purchased with varying magnifications, and a range of one of each +1, +2, +3, and +4 dioptres will give you all you should need, particularly if your housing allows you to attach more than one in whatever combination is best for the particular subject.

Exactly how best to attach them will depend very much on the housing you are using. If the housing will not allow the addition of dioptres to the camera lens in the housing then don't buy it if there is the remotest chance that you may ever want to do some serious macro work. Often the housing designer has built the housing to be such a snug fit around the camera that there is no space to screw on even an extra lens a few millimetres thick, and the opportunity to get some amazing close-up shots is totally lost – so check on this before investing in a housing.

In simple terms, a dioptre will magnify the subject but reduce the depth of field. Let me explain this. If your camera is set to focus on infinity without any additional dioptre fitted, everything from about a metre from your camera to infinity will be in focus. The more zoom you use, the closer subjects will appear to be, but the

actual distance that is in focus will be less. Add a magnifying dioptre, get close as you can to your tiny macro subject, and you will find that the actual depth of the field of focus reduces to a matter of a few centimetres, and any fractional move of the camera or of the subject that alters the distance between them will result in the subject going out of focus.

Generally speaking, the greater the degree of magnification provided by the dioptre the more limited the actual use. So a +2 dioptre will give a degree of magnification while still allowing general use for wider-angle subjects, though you may find focusing and use of auto-focus impaired due to this reduction in depth of field. Attach a +3 only when you plan only to be filming macro subjects within under a metre. Use +4 only for the most serious of macro filming such as fish eggs or pygmy seahorse, and be prepared for a minimal depth of field – the slightest variation in the distance between camera and subject will result in a loss of focus.

A +2 dioptre fitted to a lens

Generally you will only set up the camera for the higher levels of magnification when diving in the expectation of filming some tiny specific subject.

Tip | Up close and personal

Without trying to explain the optical physics of this filming formula, if you want to get maximum close up shots of a tiny sea creature the trick is to get as close to it as you can, have as high a magnification dioptre attached as you can cope with, use as great a degree of zoom as you can, and adjust focus by the tiniest movements of the camera towards or away from your subject. So this technique is a total contradiction of the advice that I gave about zoomed shots being something to avoid as they result in a loss of quality – for macro filming we break the rules

A pygmy sea horse in front of a finger! (yes, the big pink thing!). A +4 dioptre was used here.

Positioning yourself

Another piece of advice I give that horrifies divers, as it goes against all we have ever been taught, is that if you propose filming macro subjects you should carry more weight than normal. The camera must be absolutely rock solid for the shots to work. The slightest movement of the camera will be massively exaggerated at this degree of magnification, and the slightest movement will mean loss of focus. Remember that to use a shot we need to hold perfect focus and composition for several seconds which is a massive challenge when the most imperceptible camera movement will ruin the shot.

Provided the substrate allows – and most classic 'muck dives' are on a sea floor where this is possible – first of all get absolutely solid on the sea bed. Let every scrap of air out of the BC and the extra weight you are carrying will help you settle down. Inevitably this will stir up sand or silt, so be patient and wait till the snowstorm you have created has totally subsided. A rushed shot will still have swirling particles that detract from the shot's quality.

My favourite technique is to create a human tripod for the housing with my elbows firmly planted as two points of the tripod and using the sea bed or a rock as the third point of the tripod. Alternatively, if you are aiming for a specific subject, you may want to go prepared with a tripod – though remember if you do that

The 'human tripod' technique in use

you will need to carry an extra weight belt or some other way of anchoring and steadying the tripod, as without something to steady its base a tripod with housing attached may be top-heavy and unstable.

The technique can be varied for subjects that are higher up off the sea bed by using a longer legged tripod and the diver standing solid on substrate, in the same position as a tripod would be used by a photographer on land.

Obviously I would totally discourage these techniques in areas of coral growth or any other undersea life at risk of damage.

Another tip is not to press the eyepiece/viewfinder of the housing to your mask as any slight movement of the head will be transmitted to the housing. Keep your eye slightly back from the viewfinder so you can see the image without having that physical contact. This is one big advantage of external monitors – there is no need nor temptation to be glued to an eyepiece.

It hardly needs to be said that the best macro subjects are the most sedentary. So a frogfish is perhaps the ideal subject. Sitting motionless their infinite patience gives you the opportunity to film them from every angle and to get close-up shots of every part of their anatomy.

More skittish subjects are difficult to capture and here another skill comes into play – your own patience. Stay calm and motionless for long enough and virtually every creature will eventually feel less threatened by your presence and settle down, providing you with the opportunity to get your shots.

All this assumes that you and your subject can both stay immobile. If there is strong current, or any degree of surge – particularly in shallower water – accept the limitations of this technique. Unlike stills photographers, who can snap off frames in such conditions and get great results, there is virtually no chance of achieving this on film. There are 24 frames per second so to get our six to ten second chunk of footage we need to be steady for somewhere between about 150 and 240 frames compared to the stills photographer's single frame. My advice – if the conditions are not right, don't even waste your time trying!

Sometimes even the most infinite patience is not enough. No matter how motionless we think we may be, our huge cumbersome bodies straddled across the seabed, noisily breathing out bubbles, will deter the shyest sea creatures, such as garden eels from emerging.

So how do we capture images of these creatures?

How to capture garden eels on film

Think about garden eels. Forests of them sway gracefully picking tiny morsels from the current until you get anywhere near them and they disappear. No matter how patiently you wait they won't fully emerge and start feeding again until you move on – at best they will tentatively poke their heads out a small way and skittishly retract back into their burrows at the slightest movement or exhalation of air. So how do film- makers get those great shots? Here's how I do it.

When you have decided which eels you want to shoot and what your angle will be, approach the eel bed. They will of course all disappear down their burrows. Set your camera, lights and focus exactly as you want them, drape a spare weight belt over the housing to keep it exactly in position, turn on the lights, press record, and swim as far from the housing as you can while keeping it in sight. Without your disturbance in the water the eels will soon emerge and the presence of the inanimate camera will not distract them from getting back to their normal behaviour patterns.

The longer you leave the camera the better the results will be and the more choice of shots. Even if you leave it running until tape/lights/battery run out, tape is cheap, batteries recharge, and in one dive you have classic garden eel footage!

With garden eels an interesting permutation of this technique is to leave the camera set in auto-focus; as an eel emerges the camera will focus on it and as it withdraws the camera will pull focus to another eel. There will be a lot of wasted footage but among it there should be some intriguing shots as the particular eels in focus change. This is another way of using the auto-focus capabilities of the camera to good advantage.

Some examples of macro subjects

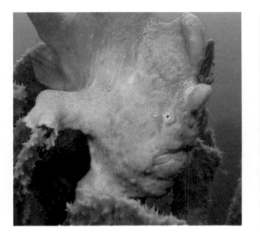 

Half and half

A creative use of the half and half shot

Some of the most striking shots that you will have seen in coffee-table books by stills photographers will be the half and half images – when half the frame is underwater and half surface. There are many permutations of this theme – dive boat on the surface with diver below, reef below and island above, blue sky above and fish below.

This technique is far easier for a stills photographer. Using a large dome port and often specialised over and under lenses they need only capture one frame. For the video cameraman the challenges are much greater but the results can be stunning.

How to achieve succesful half and half footage

A canoe over a reef makes an ideal half and half shot

1. Firstly, you need to capture a usable length of shot – around ten seconds – which is not as easy as it sounds. If you are in water where you can stand this is easier, but if not then you need amazing and precise buoyancy control and a very steady pair of hands. The two techniques vary, although in both cases flat calm water is virtually essential – anything more than a slight movement in the water will probably make the shots unusable.

   If you are in shallow water where you can touch bottom, first check that you can stand on the sea bed without causing damage to any coral that might be in the area. You will probably find it easier to do this on snorkel rather than scuba as the tanks on your back will have a destabilising effect.

2. Next get as solid as you can. This may involve loading your weight belt with far more weight than you would carry on a dive, and probably removing your fins, although this is a matter of preference as sometimes the extra surface area of the fin can actually make it easier to stand and hold a position.

   Make sure that the camera is manually focused on infinity, which on almost every camera will be confirmed by the mountains logo appearing somewhere on the visual display. If set on auto focus it will search constantly because the line created by the water surface against the lens of the housing will distract the camera.

3. Prepare the outside port of the housing as otherwise droplets of water will stick to it and lessen the impact of the shot. The easiest way to do this is in the same way that you prepare your mask for a dive – spitting on it

and then rinsing is the easiest, although I've heard of people rubbing sliced raw potatoes over theirs. Liquid products are also available to achieve the same effect including one produced to keep rain off motor cyclists visors.

Ensure you don't face the sun

4. Make sure that the sun is behind you. The reason why I stress this is that you have two completely different light levels above and below water, and to optimise the shot these levels need to be as close to each other as possible. If the light levels are too far apart – such as when shooting towards the sun – then the imbalance will be such that only one half of the shot will be clear, and of course the purpose of this technique is to be able to see both under and above water. The sun at your back may create shadow, so check to ensure that this is not cast so as to appear on the image you are shooting. If you can control the light setting of the camera from outside the housing then adjust this until the balance between the two halves of the image through the viewfinder is the best. If not, then leave the camera on auto exposure and let it find its own balance, but remember the golden rule that what you see through the viewfinder is what you will get. If using an automatic exposure it may be that slightly more of your shot will be underwater so that the camera reads the underwater light. The less the difference between the light levels under and above water the better the shot will be.

5. Remove any coloured filters as these will add an unnatural hue

6. Spend a lot of time and footage using these techniques as you then have more to choose from when it comes to editing. While actually filming you are often so preoccupied with all the logistics of setting the shot up and holding it steady that the actual content of the shot is not a main priority. It's only when reviewing the footage that you notice the tiny extra element like the fish swimming through frame or the bird overhead that makes you choose that shot above all the others.

Contrasting the world above and below

Out of your depth

If you are out of your depth then luxuries such as a firm footing and a tripod are not available to you. In these circumstances, the technique is even more difficult: although most of the ideas above are still relevant, they are just that much more difficult to apply. While some slight movement in the water can actually create an interesting effect if the camera is solidly tripod based, that same slight movement becomes just one more challenge to contend with if you are floating.

Unlike the shallow water half and half technique, when in deeper water always keep you tank and BC on. You will have a constant supply of air without being distracted by a snorkel, and more importantly you have use of the BC for fine tuning buoyancy – perfect buoyancy control is absolutely essential to get good shots. Holding the camera absolutely steady for ten seconds at a time half in and half out of the water demands impeccable control – the slightest movement of the camera will greatly detract from the impact of the shots.

7. Try lots of angles – there is no rule that says a half and half should be an exact mathematic ratio of over and under shots. Up to two thirds of one or the other can often work. Also consider camera angles – the camera does not need to be exactly horizontal – pointing slightly down or up can alter the perspective and centre of focus and will also give interesting effects. For example, if you are trying to focus attention on the land then the camera titling slightly upwards will give the effect of waves. If the reef rather than the land is the principal point of interest, then point the camera slightly downwards and allow the underwater proportion of the image be greater than half the screen.

Be creative. Half and half shots can have enormous impact

Three legs good

In shallow water you can also use the best tool of all for this technique – a tripod. If using a tripod take an extra weight belt with as much lead as you can to spread around the legs of the tripod in order to give it stability in the water.

There are two other shots worth trying.

The first of these is what I call the 'under surface' shot. It is not actually a half-and-half shot, but is the technique of filming just below the surface of the water catching the reflective surface from below. Again try different angles – slightly looking up towards the sun, towards someone looking down from the boat, or looking up towards palm trees or rocks. At night the moon or lights of the boat taken from just under the surface can make a stunning shot. Make sure that you remain just inches below the water surface to get the best effect. Try many different angles and proportions of water/surface in the frame.

Another pleasing effect is to keep the camera horizontal just under the water surface so that the underside of the surface becomes the 'sky' in the shot and then follow a diver swimming back to the boat ladder and exiting the water. These are just ideas – you will think of many variations on this theme. Not only do they make intriguing and different images in themselves, but when you come to edit they can be invaluable shots to use to round off a sequence.

The second variation is the 'breaking surface' shot. This is much the same as the under surface shot but this time breaking through the surface towards whatever you were filming, such as hands reaching down from the boat or palm trees on an island. Obviously, instead of the camera being horizontal, it will be tilted upwards at the best angle to get the shot.

When you let your imagination run there is an almost endless list of shots to which these techniques can apply. How about a diver entering the water, a child swimming on the surface, a fisherman hauling his nets or pots, or a dug-out canoe passing by. And don't overlook the opportunity offered by hotel swimming pools for getting some great and unusual shots, or for simply working on your technique.

Now, if you really want to do some funky shooting, try combining lights with half-and-half filming. If in shallow water, using flexible lights bent downwards or even lights unattached to the camera but held by an assistant can add that infill to the underwater portion of the film, particularly if close in the underwater foreground is a rock or reef that the lights can pick out. Using a similar technique at night can create some stunning results. I'm not even going to try and give guidelines for this technique as every situation will be different. But imagine, for example, a well lit dive boat or pier in the foreground and the shallow reef picked out by your lights below. There are unlimited applications of these techniques.

Frame 1: Rising…   Frame 2: hitting the surface   Frame 3: Breaking the surface

Slo-mo

When editing, if there is some movement in the water, try slow motioning the images – this can convert an unpleasant choppiness in the image to a smooth and emotive effect.

Filming at night

I'm assuming that you're comfortable with diving at night because until you are there's no point in taking a camera down – with the added distraction of a camera you'll simply become a liability to yourself and everyone else in the water!

So working on that assumption, firstly before going diving remember to do two things – set the light setting of the camera to artificial light, and remove any coloured filters.

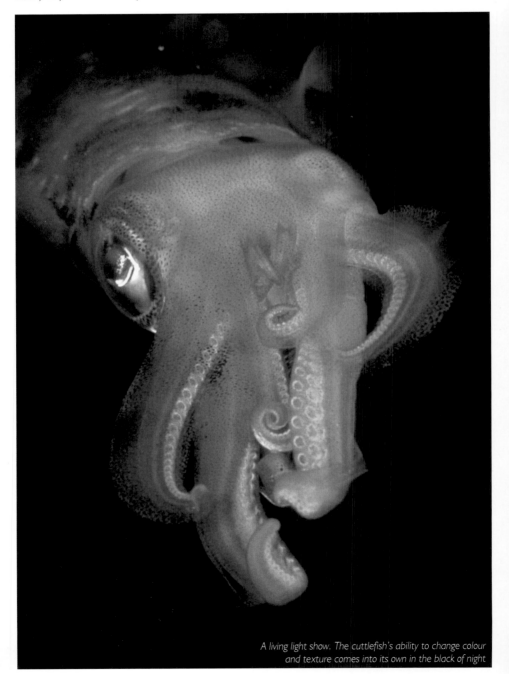

A living light show. The cuttlefish's ability to change colour and texture comes into its own in the black of night

Light configuration

The first difficulty with filming at night is that you don't have enough hands! You need one hand to hold the torch, two hands to hold the camera and work the controls, and at least one more hand to manipulate and angle the lights and work the switches.

Some housings are constructed with integral lights that are controlled from the housing arms which simplify things slightly. Combining use of the torch and housing is something that you will have to work out for yourself as the number of combinations of housings and torches is too many to try and cover. However here are two useful tips. If there is a way that the torch can be attached to your housing without impairing your use of either this is a neat solution – a small compact torch attached to a flexible arm can make life easier. If this is not an option then at the very least get a torch that can be easily turned on and off with one hand – it's surprising how many underwater torches have such complex mechanisms for turning them on and off that two hands are needed. Safety catches, inaccessible switches, or on/off mechanisms that require you to hold the torch in one hand while twisting it with the other – all of these render such torches totally impractical for the underwater cameraman.

Diver's torch fixed to housing for ease of use at night

Detail of bracket

Avoid over lighting

The key to successful night filming is to get a perfect balance of lighting. The main fault with most underwater video shot at night is over lighting – the impulse to try and light the subject as brightly as possible. At night lighting systems with a dimmer switch facility come into their own. Subtle increases or reductions in the power of the lights can make a good shot great.

Over lighting creates its own problems. If too much light is used the image can look just as if it was shot by day. A brightly lit shot of an octopus crawling over a reef at night can be hard to differentiate between the same shot by day. If shooting wide angle this is not too much of a problem the area outside the beam of the light will clearly be dark. However always remember that you are trying to tell a story, and if the story is of the octopus emerging from his lair to hunt the reef by night, then make sure that at least in setting the scene there is a wide-angle shot that clearly establishes that it is right time before moving in to the closer fully lit shots of the octopus. Never forget you are a story teller and the images must tell the story.

When filming closer shots of the subject at night your lights are the only light source, whereas by day they simply complement the ambient light to bring out colour and add fill in. So avoid over-lighting the subject as otherwise the shots will appear bleached and there will be excessive white reflection back from the subject. Looking through the viewfinder or at the screen you can easily recognise over-lighting from the reflective white spots. As I've said so often, don't just look through the viewfinder, recognise what you are seeing and take action to remedy it, as what you see there is what you will see on the television screen at home – there is no magic in the camera that will make it better. If you would like some help in recognising this problem and if your camera has a zebra mode then the same advice applies as filming during the day – use it.

A turtle caught at night

Experimental night lighting

Many night creatures are red in colour. The reason for this is that red being the colour of the spectrum that first disappears underwater, this colouring renders them virtually invisible in the night time sea.

Equally many creatures of the night ocean are very sensitive to light and will disappear if suddenly their environment becomes brightly lit. Bright lights shone at creatures at night can also temporarily blind them so sensitive are they to light, and so finely attuned are their eyes to enable them to see and hunt in the black of night.

To capture the natural behaviour of these creatures, subtle lighting is required. Many underwater stills photographers place a red filter over their spotting light or torch so as not to disturb creatures they are trying to photograph and it is a tip that we can learn from. Using a red light until ready to film will not disturb the natural behaviour of the specific animal until the video lights are turned on.

Taking this concept one stage further, in certain situations with the shyest of creatures a weak red filter over the actual video lights and proper use of white balance can produce the results you are seeking.

Red: a cloak of invisibility at night

Lights out

Tape over any record light on the camera otherwise this light may reflect onto the interior of the glass port of the housing and all your night shots will have a red light showing on them.

Avoiding back scatter

Silt, sand, and muck that you or other divers have kicked up is an even greater problem at night when every particle will reflect back at you creating horrendous backscatter. By day particles in the water can be a problem. At night they ruin the shot, as the amount of reflection caused by the lights glinting off every particle will make footage useless. The only ways to avoid this are to control your diving so that the least debris is churned up, and be patient and wait for it to settle or clear as the current washes it away. If the water is being churned up by reasons beyond your control such as surge or current, face the fact that the conditions are not ideal and just do the best that you can.

One other hint for reducing backscatter is not to light the subject head on. If you have flexible arms, bend them so that lighting is coming from the side rather than the front as this will reduce the amount of reflection off particles. If your lights can be detached from the housing this gives even more scope for angling the light to reduce the scatter effect.

One problem of filming at night in many parts of the tropics is the life attracted to the cameras. Krill, worms, and all sorts of zooplankton can be drawn to the lights to the extent that the hailstorm of living scuirming creatures swarming around the lights makes filming impossible. There is only one solution. Extinguish all lights and sit in total darkness until the swarm has dispersed - though when you turn on the lights again the swarm will gradually return.

Krill: the night time film makers 'enemy'

Artificial light white balance

If you cannot access the white balance control through the housing, ensure that the camera is set to artificial light before every night dive.

Dim and dimmer

One set of lights that I use has a dimmer switch on the batteries so that I can select the light level and achieve the best light balance. In my view every underwater lighting system should have such a facility. If yours doesn't then there are three ways to try to reduce over-lighting the subject which are effectively the same techniques that you would use by day:

1. Increase the distance between camera and subject by backing off until the best balance is attained.
2. If you have flexible arms, keeping the camera in the same position draw the arms back so they are further from the subject and casting a wider and therefore more diffused beam.
3. Change the angle either of the lights or of the camera or both so that if reflection is coming off a particular part of the subject this is reduced. Direct light blasting at the subject from close range is far more likely to cause hot spots of light than more subtly directed lighting.

Creatures of the night

Bobbit worm

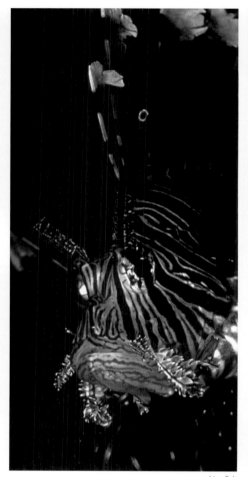

Hairy frogfish and lure

Lionfish

Hunting octopus - wide angle...

...and close up

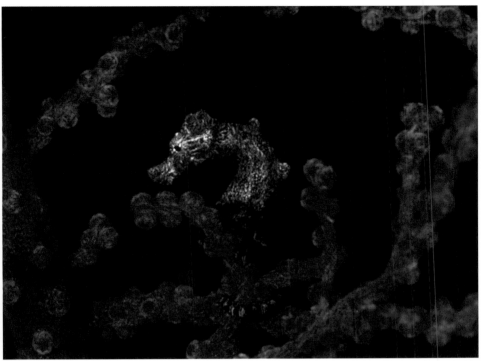

Pygmy seahorse at night

Moray eel

Stargazer

Tip | **Out of your depth**

Shadow can also detract from the quality of footage shot at night and the same rules apply – actually look and see what the image looks like through the viewfinder and unless you are deliberately trying to create a shadow effect, alter the angle of lighting and filming to minimise the area of shadow. So often a shot will have one side of the frame showing one side of the subjects face brightly lit with the other half of the frame and subject virtually blacked out.

Blenny

9. Making a film

Producing a film in whatever format you choose is the culmination of your work as a videographer. So before even starting to try and produce a film, it is essential to learn as much as you can by watching analytically the work of others, not as a piece of entertainment, but to critique how the whole film is put together. So many of us watch television uncritically throughout our lives without appreciating and understanding the techniques that make a programme watchable.

Try to visit to an underwater film festival and talk to the people there who have actually produced the films. In the splendid solitude of your own home, editing away in your study or bedroom, you may think your films looks great and works well. Go and watch a selection of the works of people who have already done it, listen to the comments and criticisms of those around you, and learn by the mistakes of others. We've all been there and made the mistakes – I certainly have! I'm just showing you how to avoid them.

Editing techniques

Editing is part of the total package of underwater filming. Creating a final product that can be enjoyed and that tells a story will not only give the satisfaction of entertaining and educating others, but will teach you a lot about filming. Learning which shots work and why, and how to improve your technique, will make you a far better cameraman.

Edit in camera

The most basic form of editing is to edit in camera and this means exactly what it says – you film the whole piece to a script you have already worked out. It's the story of a classic day's diving. The camera tape is the final version of the film that you can then play back through the television in the bar later or from which you can run off copies. It's uncomplicated, fun to do, and great to share with the others, but that is as far as it goes. Do it and enjoy it, but one tip – exercise great self control in the shots you are actually taking because what you film is what you get as the end result. If you have sections that are out of focus, shots that don't work, or the film just drags on, then it becomes a bore rather than fun to watch – keep it tight. Edits in camera are one time that the review function on a housing may come in useful to delete shots as you go along if that function can be accessed through the housing.

An edit in camera is the simplest form of telling a story with your camera. Dive stores often do a variation on this theme. For example, if you are diving Stingray City in Grand Cayman they may start and end the video they sell you with previously shot and edited sequences of the stingrays, and drop into the middle some shots of your actual dive filmed that day. This is how many professionals at dive stores churn out the tapes that they have for sale at the end of every diving day.

Shot list

1. Cars arriving at dock, unloading and getting into boat

2. Shot from boat looking back as we leave the dock

3. Everyone kitting up

4. Divers getting into water – first from surface then from below

5. Descending to the wreck

6. Wide angle shots of the wreck

7. Closer shots of the wreck with and without other divers mixed with…

8. … Closer shots of the other divers

8. Surfacing

9. Heading back to the dock

10 Sunset

A shooting script may look like this.

The Golden Rule of Editing

Never forget – you are a story teller, and the overall combination of images, words, music and effects are brought together for that one single reason – to tell your story and entertain your audience.

Studio editing

The more common understanding of editing is when you select your best shots and re-arrange them into a piece, adding titles, music, sound effects, and narration or at least a combination of these. A few years ago this would involve buying another expensive item of equipment, an editing desk, but now editing packages are available that enable you to edit a film on just about every home computer. The range of editing equipment available extends from cheap packages for the home PC up to fully professional digital editing suites is so vast and such a rapidly changing market that I won't try to review it in this book. However there is something available to suit every budget, so seek advice and shop around for the package that best suits your requirements.

The final option is to take your footage to a professional editor or studio – great if you can afford it. If this is your route then go as fully prepared as you can – know your storyline and have the shots pre- selected as far as you are able. Most studios charge by the hour or by the day, so the less of their time you are buying the better. You should be guaranteed a high quality product – but at a price. If you have hopes of achieving broadcast sales of your film, this may be the only way of achieving a product of sufficient quality to pass broadcaster's stringent controls.

Working with a professional editor can have extra benefits. From time to time divers of varying levels of experience and ability have rented my edit suite for a couple of days to sit with Fionn and myself to produce a piece from their camera tapes, whether as a short contest entry, a show reel of their best footage, a present for a friend or a souvenir for themselves or their club of a trip or dive. Without exception they have gone away knowing far more about how to film and what shots to look for next time. You will always learn by working with others.

Whatever the route, editing is a painful process, as you see your own footage far differently to an independent viewer. While a particular shot may mean a very great deal to you, does it say anything to anyone watching the final film? Maybe you only got this shot after a very long and difficult dive, maybe you spent weeks of searching before you found that nudibranch, maybe that distant blur was the first shark you had ever seen or that tiny blob in centre screen is a tiny baby octopus – no matter how emotionally attached you are to the shot, if it doesn't work then you have to scrap it.

A typical editing suite

Effects

Most edit packages contain a number of different effects. Some of these can be extremely useful.

Perhaps the most useful of all is the dissolve. This is where instead of one shot ending and the next starting in the next frame, which can sometimes appear abrupt, the two shots flow into one another by the new shot gradually appearing over the old shot and the old shot then fading out. Used properly this can make images flow smoothly into one another and take away the abruptness of the cut between two shots. The length of the dissolve – the number of frames that if covers – will depend on the effect you are trying to create. A short dissolve of only a few

frames will be virtually imperceptible to a viewer but will serve to smooth what may otherwise have been an abrupt move from one image to the next. Longer dissolves can produce an almost dream-like feel to a piece. When you get familiar with your editing package you should also experiment with the positioning of the dissolve. Sometimes it is most effective if positioned immediately over the cut between the two shots. Other times positioning it further into one or other shot can give an impression of that shot fading in or out.

Slow motion shots can be useful in creating a feel to a sequence. Colour correction can also help to blend shots together which may have been shot in

A dissolve over four frames

A split screen effect can show different aspects at the same time

different conditions. Also there are a range of other effects that will create all types of links between shots or sections of the film. Picture in picture and split screen effects are just two of many that if used properly can add to the quality of the film. Get to know the full capabilities of your editing package and try out combinations of more than one effect.

Professionally produced titling and appropriate use of maps and other graphics can greatly enchance the overall quality of the film.

However, tread cautiously and avoid over using effects unless they actually improve the film by their presence. There is a temptation if you have an effects package to over-use it.

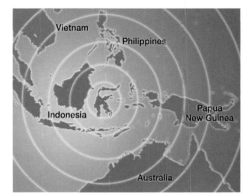

Maps and graphics help ground the film in reality

Slow motion is a highly effective means of creating atmosphere

Professional titling sets the right tone for your film

These sharks were superimposed using the picture-in-picture effect

Effects

Too many effects, or the use of inappropriate effects, can ruin a good film. The same applies with captions, title sequences and sound effects. Don't regard editing as a chance to show off how clever you are, as this will only intrude into the film and detract from what may otherwise be a good story with good images.

Never use the effects package in the camera. Save these for the editing process when you can make a considered judgement as to whether or not a particular effect works, rather than being committed to it as it is an effect on the camera master tape.

Some of the type of effects to avoid can be seen opposite: a bar and sawtooth effect. These effects might be acceptable on a home video but when creating professional films for sale and broadcast they come across as amateur. Watch wildlife programmes on the television, as well as other types of films, documentaries and programming to see how other film makers use effects to join sections of film, create story-telling moments or to add 'pace' to the film.

Examples of effects to avoid

If in doubt, stick to dissolves, quick editing or a section of black frames to denote a change of scene.

Sound effects

We take the everyday background sounds of life so much for granted that they are often over-looked by film makers. Build a library of sounds such as general wave noise, outboard engines, sea birds, and water noises such as waves and splashing sounds. Keep these sound effects on a dedicated tape or CD somewhere. Background sounds can add considerable atmosphere to a film and are great to have in stock for other projects.

Most housings will record sound. However, when you listen to the sound of an actual dive played back in the studio you will be surprised just how much background noise there is underwater. The microphone may pick up the sound of other divers breathing, creaking sounds as you adjust lighting arms or controls, divers banging tanks, movement in the water, and a general clicking sound heard at many tropical destinations of fish feeding on coral – a surprising cacophony of sounds. You may find that the sound recorded while you were actually diving may not create exactly the mellow relaxed underwater ambience that you were looking to achieve. A session in a swimming pool – with the pool filters turned off! - when you record your own breathing at different rates and levels, may provide you with all the breathing sounds you will need for future projects, and will add another layer to your productions.

26 or 52 minutes?

Although television slots are either 30 or 60 minutes, all programmes to fit these half hour or hour slots should be a maximum length of either 26 or 52 minutes to allow for commercial breaks and announcements. If making a 52 minute long film ensure there is a natural break after 26 minutes in case a broadcaster decides to screen it in two parts.

Music

Music can add greatly to the atmosphere of a film, and well chosen music can greatly compliment the actual images. However, at all costs avoid the cliched but typical new age 'underwater' music that most video makers feel is essential. Nothing can spoil the impact of good images more than pan-pipe elevator muzak!

Equally avoid using a couple of your favourite songs simply because you like them unless they have a very clear link to the images, which is generally highly unlikely. You may like both the images and the music, but it rarely if ever works for others watching the film. Often simple sound effects, long sustained notes, simple pulses or beats, or even the sound of regular breathing underwater are all that is needed to add atmosphere and so enhance the impact of the images.

Breaks between sequences

Most films will be constructed of a number of compartments. For example there may be the octopus section, the shark section, the night section... Make sure that these do not just run into each other. Signify the end of a sequence by some clear device such as a new title, a freeze frame, or even just a fade to black for a couple of seconds so the viewer appreciates that we are now moving on to new ground.

Listen to editors

In my first film *'Caymania'* there is one shot of a stingray that is over a minute in length. I was so proud that I had managed to follow the ray and keep it in focus for so long that I believed anyone watching the film would be overwhelmed by my skill and prowess as a cameraman. Looking at the film now, a clip of ten seconds of the very best section of the shot would have been more than enough, but I was so proud of the shot and so attached to it that my self indulgence over-rode the editor's advice.

Surface intervals

Even to the biggest fish fanatic, an hour of relentless fish footage would be overkill! So ensure that you film enough surface footage to provide an interesting interlude to your underwater footage.

A sequence like that left, showing divers entering the water to film shoaling Barracuda can benefit from occasional 'top-side' shots of the next divers getting in or preparing their dive gear on deck. Footage of simple day-to-day diving activities can act as your own personal stock image library to add colour and life to your films.

Cutaways

As soon as you start editing you will appreciate the importance and value of 'cutaway' shots. A cutaway may not in itself be a particularly special shot but is invaluable to you in telling the story in an edit. It is the device that you use to move from one shot to another smoothly.

For example, you wish to show two very different fish shot on different days at different locations when the light and colour of the two shots are very different. If you run one shot immediately after the other they would appear disjointed. But if you split them up using a cutaway such as a diver's face, then the shots will flow smoothly and the fact they do not match up will not be apparent

to the viewer. In fact on every dive trip I have a session of filming 'pointing' shots when I film my buddy in every possible way - swimming towards the camera and away from it, wide angle pointing up and down to the left and right, and close up shots of him turning his head, his eyes moving as if looking at something or following it's movement. It's amazing how useful these shots can be and the extent to which they help an edit.

The use of a cutaway – frame 2 in the sequence below – of the smaller fish allows one to build a sequence of the frogfish and slice together a frogfish shot with and without additional fish

The cutaway of the catfish not only progresses the story but helps us move smoothly from the close up of the frogfish to a similar wider shot

Narration

If the presenter is to be on-screen and speaking to the camera this will restrict sales to anything but your own language. If there is narration without 'talking heads' on screen, there is the possibility of sales in countries where the narration can be dubbed in other languages.

The current vogue is very much in favour of presenter led programmes, of which there are two distinct styles, the old-fashioned approach of the presenter talking to camera and telling the story, and the participating presenter who is very much in the thick of things and becomes a part of the show. If you are lucky enough to be

commissioned to produce a programme in this style then go for it! However if you are funding the production yourself in the hope of achieving sales, then both types of talking head presentation are to be avoided. Narration that tells the story without the narrator ever talking to camera means that your film will be far more marketable worldwide. Even some film festivals and contests may ask for a dub of the film without narration, together with a time-coded script, so that the entries in their contest can all be enjoyed in that country's native language.

Script writing

Script writing is a skill in itself. We have all watched countless documentaries on television, but rarely consider just how difficult writing a script actually is. Yet no matter how stunning the images may be, without the cement of the script

to tie everything together, a film will fail to entertain its audience. It's a skill that cannot be taught in this book, but a few hints as to what not to do might help.

Above all avoid lists – simply naming a

succession of sea creatures one after the other is the surest way to lose an audience. If your film is indeed simply a succession of images of different fish strung together for no other reason than that you are proud of the shots, then you have missed the point of film-making, namely telling a story. It can be hard in the edit suite discarding what you know to be excellent shots of a wide variety of fish, but that should not be a reason for their inclusion.

Likewise avoid describing what is happening on the screen unless a description is essential to your viewers understanding of an unusual behaviour or phenomenon. So the words that accompany the sequence of images that showed the octopus squeezing into a broken bottle (image above) were not:

"And here is an octopus squeezing into an old bottle"

but

"Even man's debris comes into play in the struggle between detection and camouflage".

Try and apply a technique known as 'talking off the picture'. The viewer can see what is happening on screen and does not need to be told, so instead tell them something that progresses the story against the backdrop of the images they are seeing.

Well placed humour also appeals to viewers and helps to bind a script together. This can also be visual humour if the person or creature in shot is in themselves amusing.

Avoid repetition. Using the same words over and over again can be extremely irritating for a viewer. So, for example, instead of continuously saying "underwater" use variations such as "in these waters", "below the surface", "in the seas", "in the ocean"…

And don't be afraid of letting the images tell their own story. Less is often better than more, understatement better than overstatement. If the footage is spectacular, entertaining, or intriguing you don't need to tell people this – it should be obvious from what they are seeing. First time film makers often seem to have a compulsion to cover every moment of footage with narration. This is not necessary and if you study the films of some of the great documentary producers you may be surprised how minimal the narration is at times.

I find that I have a general idea of the story I wish to tell and the sequences and images I want to include, so usually start an edit with a rough outline script of where I am going. The script then evolves during the course of the edit – often straying a very long way from my initial concept.

Basking Shark

10. Selling your work

I believe that gathering dust on many divers shelves is stunning footage that really ought to be seen by a wider audience – great shots, unique and unusual behaviour, strange and bizarre creatures. The difficulty is getting that footage, or the film that you have edited, screened on television. Despite the proliferation of new terrestrial and satellite broadcasters, it is still very hard for an outsider to break into the world of television. I have spent many years trying to get my name and my work established so there is at least a degree of recognition by broadcasters when they are presented with my latest production, yet I still feel I have a lot to learn.

The television business

What every film-maker dreams of is a commission. You come up with an idea, pitch it to a television station who like the idea and agree to fund it, and you head off to a remote destination with the budget covered and being paid a daily rate for your work. Unfortunately, dreams such as this don't often come true. I was once told that more than 99% of all proposals to television stations end up in the bin, and from my own experiences I can well believe this.

It is also true that while in the recent past television stations appeared to have unlimited pools of cash to fund the making of documentaries, this is rarely now the case. Unless state funded, television is a business like any other. Revenue comes either by subscription as is the case with many movie channels so that films can be shown uninterrupted by commercial breaks, or in the majority of cases from advertising revenue. As the number of satellite, digital and cable television channels increases, viewers are spread more widely between all the channels and advertising revenue is similarly thinly spread.

But it is still possible to get commissioned and there is an accepted procedure that you must follow to even have a chance of your proposal being considered.

The pitch (see example right)

Firstly find out from your target television station the full name and contact details of the commissioning editor. It's only a small touch, but a pitch addressed by name is far better than a general 'Dear Sir' – particularly if the commissioning editor is female!

The pitch should be no longer than one A4 sheet of paper which you will fax or email to the commissioning editor. It is your one hope for the proposal, so you can never spend too much time fine tuning it. It is your sales pitch and you want to put forward your proposal in its best light. You are fishing for funding and this is the lure. Try and target the proposal to fit the style and programming schedule of the channel. If you think it would fit into a particular scheduling slot, say so. Most of all, keep your proposals crisp, precise and short. Here are the main points you should cover in your proposal:

1. Start with the title and a technical description of the programme you are offering. A catchy title helps but if it is too obscure you should include an explicit subtitle. Maybe follow up the title with a quotation or an anecdote – what print journalists call 'colour'. It might capture the imagination of the commissioning editor or give them a flavour of what is to follow. However, if you are not sure about the impact of the quote/anecdote, don't do it. For example, I pitched my 'Ocean Oases' series in the following way.

Ocean Oases. Six x 30 minute underwater documentaries filmed at some of the planet's remotest islands. 6 tiny dots scattered around the globe, each with it's own undersea life, each still virtually untouched by the modern world. Once all the world's oceans were like this.

2. First paragraph. This is the most important information on the page. Many people will not read beyond this, so be sure it clearly states what your film is about. There is a general view in television that if you cannot explain what your film is about in a few sentences, you cannot make a coherent film.

3. Briefly explain the location(s) of the film. The time-scale, when do you want to shoot, how long will it take and when can you deliver. What will we actually see? Give an idea of the scenes you are hoping to shoot and subjects you are going to film.

4. Do you have anything special that could be advertised as 'For the first time' such as unusual creatures or behaviour that has never been filmed before, or a new angle on an old story. Any impressive talent associated with the project such as the narrator or musical composer. If you or your crew are award winning, say so.

5. What is the style of shooting? Is your film observational and hand-held or highly stylised and beautifully lit? Or is it something in between? Will you use conventional interview techniques or simply capture conversations on the run? Is there music, specially composed or recorded? Will there be a presenter? If so, who? As regards presentation think carefully about your target audience.

6. Why do you want to make this film?

The 'critters' Trilogy
(3 x 30 minute documentaries or 1 x 90 minutes)

A three-part visual feast depicting the planet's strangest sea creatures
and their even stranger habits.
Like aliens from a distant planet, they indulge in bizarre mating rituals and
display ingenious hunting methods with a vast array of cunning weaponry
and unrivalled camouflage skills.
But how and why did they evolve like this?
The 'critters' Trilogy provides compelling evidence of nature's most extraordinary
skills at adaptation, including among many others...

- The gormless-looking frogfish with the fastest bite in the sea
- Slugs that produce their own deadly chemical weapons
- Sea creatures that hunt with lethal spears
- The world's tiniest fighting sea horses

The product of many years scouring the planet's oceans, the 'critters' trilogy
reveals images rarely and often never seen on television
Filmed on DV and produced by Shark Bay Films, winners of an
unprecedented double Palme d'Or at the Antibes World Underwater Film Festival

Available Summer 2003
PLEASE WATCH TASTER CD -
IT'S ONLY 5 MINUTES LONG
Contact:
John Boyle john@sharkbayfilms.demon.co.uk

The next stage

Rejections come back pretty quickly, sometimes even the same day, and are usually a simple one line e-mail. Don't be disheartened by rejections. There are all kinds of reasons why they might not want the idea. Maybe they are already working on a similar project, they did something similar last year; it does not fit the profile of the channel, or they have no suitable slot. Maybe it is a great idea but the timing is wrong. Don't give up, re-write the pitch and try again in a few month's time.

But if the lure has worked and the commissioning editor is interested in your idea, he or she will either ask you to come in and talk about the idea or ask for a more detailed treatment.

The words 'proposal' and 'treatment' are often confused. Strictly speaking, a proposal is a simple description of the film or programme you are proposing to make. A treatment is a detailed description, ideally explaining the project scene by scene. It will be several pages long, possibly more. Often the broadcaster when asking you for more information will have guidelines for you to follow, known as 'Invitations to Tender'. Always read them very carefully to make sure that you are not going into too little or too much detail.

This is your chance to present more fully the story you want to tell.

Make it interesting and cover all the highlights that were mentioned in your initial pitch in fuller detail. Include a page about yourselves, your experience, qualifications, and other productions you have worked on.

If you have won awards, list them. If you have made past television sales, list them too. A show reel of your best work to date can also be useful and may actually be requested.

At this stage you will also have to produce a budget – see the sample below

Finally, if you get that commission, read the contract carefully. You may find that the rights in the film pass exclusively to the commissioning station. Make sure you understand fully what you are signing.

Draft Budget

Filming Budget

Filming xx days for 2 cameramen @ xx per day £

Rental of xx full underwater filming units including:
cameras
underwater housings
lighting equipment
@ xx per day
for xx days £

Tape costs xx camera tapes £

Travel to location £

Accommodation £

Subsistence £

Insurances £

Total £

Editing Budget

Edit and master tapes £

Rental edit suite xx days @ £xx per day £

Editor xx days @ £xx per day £

Script writing £

Narrators fee £

Sound recording and sound studio £

Postage, phones, couriers, stationery etc £

Secretarial £

Music £

Graphic £

Miscellaneous expenses £

Total £

Add together both totals £

Total budget = £

Grant aid

Many countries and regions have Film Councils which control a substantial pool of grant funding from central government and other sources. This can take many forms ranging from simple loans to finance production, often repayable from the first sales of the film and with interest and other conditions attaching, to non-repayable grants. These may be targeted at specific sectors of the film industry and will have very specific requirements, but are certainly worth investigating.

Self funding

Self funding means you go out and make your film and then try to sell it. This is the route that most small independent film producers follow. While once you have produced a film you can try to sell it direct to television stations this is a very difficult and time consuming route to take. If you could not get the broadcaster interested in a one page fax or email outline of the project, it is unlikely to wade through the piles of unsolicited tapes it receives every day. So you may wish to appoint a television agent to sell your work for you while you concentrate on the actual film production.

Television agents

Agents rates vary between ten and 35%, and in addition there will be expenses incurred on your behalf that they will seek to recoup from sales revenue, so again read the contract very carefully and be prepared to haggle over terms. Agents will also invariably require an exclusivity agreement, which allows them all sales in all media worldwide for a specific period. If for example you want the rights to sell video or DVD copies of your work, make sure the contract reserves this right for you.

In return however, you get the benefit of the agent's contacts throughout the television world, their knowledge of potential purchasers of your programmes that you have never heard of, and their attendance at television trade shows around the world. In some cases you can also benefit from the inclusion of your film in a larger deal. Many stations will have a shopping list and for example be looking for a certain number of hours of nature programmes – your film could be added as part of a package and a sale made that otherwise would not have happened.

Don't forget that the agent only gets paid if they make a sale so they will be pushing your film for you to every possible potential buyer.

Organising your shots – Shot lists

If you have collected a variety of good shots, then it is pointless having them gather dust on the shelf at home. There are other ways of making money from your footage, and the most common is from selling individual shots. But before being in a position to sell footage it needs to be in good order.

The whole point of this exercise is to be able to find shots at some time in the future when you may have hundreds of tapes containing many hours of footage from many destinations. What if someone wants to buy a shot, or you need something for an edit you are doing, or simply want to show your mates that great shark shot or what a frogfish really looks like – how will you be able to find it?

It may seem a drag at the time, something that you think you will leave till you get home, but try and get in the discipline of shot listing any completed tapes at the end of every day.

When you start a new tape, label the tape box and attach the sticky label to the cassette itself. Use a simple system – *Red Sea, Tape 1* is all that you need – too complicated a labelling system gets confusing.

Shot descriptions

Keep the shot description as concise as you can, but remember that it should be sufficient to identify the shot in years to come when memories are not quite so fresh. *'Angelfish'* may not be enough – in time you may have hundreds of shots of angelfish and will not want to trawl through all of them to locate something specific.
Wide angle of angelfish panning from left to right then zooming in to close up of head, is far more use, but also far too long. So try to use an intelligible shorthand that you apply consistently in your logging.
There are some abbreviations commonly used in the film industry that are universally understood: **w/a** – wide angle, **c/u** – close up, **l/r** – moving from left to right
And you can always add some of your own. So the angelfish shot could now read: *'Angelfish w/a l/r to c/u head'*

Below is an example of a shot list.

Location	Date	Tape	Subject	Quality
Loloata, PNG	20.05.03	01:00:00	Mantis shrimp w/a	***
Loloata, PNG	20.05.03	01:00:48	Mantis shrimp c/u eye	****
Loloata, PNG	20.05.03	01:01:29	Jawfish in hole w/a &c/u	***
Loloata, PNG	20.05.03	01:02:52	Nudibranch mating sequence	***
Loloata, PNG	20.05.03	01:06:23	Yellow frogfish on sponge	***
Loloata, PNG	20.05.03	01:07:00	Same frogfish c/u eyes and mouth	****
Loloata, PNG	20.05.03	01:09:25	Same frogfish catches small fish	*****

The first digits under the Tape heading identify the tape itself, in this case tape 01 from this shoot. The next two sets of digits are minutes and seconds. This index number will be the start point of the shot; there is no need to log the end point of a shot, as it is the beginning of the next.

The quality is simply your own grading system. I use stars, one being poor and five excellent. If you have a computer, log the shots on there. Then if in years to come you need to find an angelfish shot, simply execute a search and all your angelfish shots will be fully described to enable you to make an immediate selection.

Stock shots

Until you become well known there is little chance of being contacted with an enquiry for footage, so most film-makers use the services of a stock shots library. There are stock shots agents in most countries that specialise in providing shots on request. Generally they will have a broad base, few specialise exclusively in even as wide a category as exclusively nature shots, and generally underwater shots will be a speciality that they don't often get asked for.

Before agreeing to take on your shots the agent will need to see what you have to offer. Send a time coded and shot listed VHS with shot description and location. Use a professional approach. Never send your original camera tapes to an agent at any time. If they agree to take your shots, you will need to provide a master in Beta SP format, again well labelled and shot listed. This shot list will be more detailed than your own, as it must describe fully to a buyer what the shot will show and where it was shot. Buyers from stock agencies rely on the written description to pre-select shots they may wish to view and a poorly described shot may not even get looked at. So our earlier angel fish shot would now be described *'Brightly coloured angel fish, good light, clear blue water and white sand. Caribbean. Variety of w/a and c/u shots'.*

Stock agents usually take around 50% of income from sales and they will usually want exclusive rights to your shots. Try to avoid this exclusivity clause if you can, as the more agents hold your work the better the chance of a sale. Many potential buyers of stock shots such as advertising executives will not usually shop around. They will have a number of favoured agencies whom they will instruct to source footage for them, which is another good reason to have your work with as many agents as possible to increase the chances of a sale. Stock agents have a scale of prices for footage that will depend on the eventual use.

Don't expect miracles from stock sales. You will usually get contacted with very specific requests that you just cannot meet, but learn by that and when filming shoot what you think might be a saleable stock shot. Any sale generated by having your footage with a stock library is a sale that would not have been made if your shots were simply sitting on the shelf at home.

I have sold footage through stock agents which has been used on game shows, television adverts, and corporate productions as well as in documentaries made by other producers. Perhaps the two strangest requests to date were that I produce a loop tape of shark footage that would be the backdrop behind the chairman of a large public company announcing the annual results; and a request for *'wobbly bright coloured sea creatures'* for a music video.

Tip Key words

The point of the shotlist is to be able to find shots that you need with the greatest of ease by using the search tool on your computer. So when logging these on ensure that you use key words and spell them correctly! Ensure that all night shots have the word night in the description.

Don't use differing names for creatures such as sometimes putting frogfish and sometimes froggy... and keep your search terms simple, so if searching for frogfish simply search for frog and it will trigger both.

Trade exchange

Some dive boats and destinations may be willing to do a trade exchange deal. They provide you with free diving/accommodation and you in return supply them with footage, or produce a short promotional film for them. This is the very first step on the ladder for many underwater film- makers, as when you have done this once you have far more credibility to approach others. But how do you persuade that first operation that your work is good enough that you will produce a quality product for them? You do this by having a show reel for them to see.

Promotional shot for the diveboat FeBrina

Show reels

So, you want to persuade a dive boat or resort that you're the person to make their new promotional video. You want to give a talk at your kids school or to a local group. You want to persuade a working film-maker to take you along on a trip as their assistant. You have an idea for a film or other project and you want to get some backing, or at least persuade an airline/tour operator/tourist board to cut you a good deal. You need to show people that you are serious about your underwater videography. Or you just want to impress your friends. Then you need to prepare a show reel.

Simply putting your best shots on a tape is not enough. Edit some sequences together, keep them short and only include the absolute best material – a couple of weak shots can destroy the whole impact. Generate titles before each sequence, and leave a section of black tape between each. Add music if you wish, as this may enhance the impact of the show reel. Make it look as good and professional as you can, as this will become the shop window for your work.

Contests

Another way of getting interest in your work and possibly generating sales or commissions is by entering the contest circuit.

The table shows a list of some of the annual contests that are worth considering entering. The list is far from exhaustive and includes only specific underwater film festivals. Searches on the Internet will come up with many more and other more general wildlife contests are worth investigating. Some are big international events, others smaller.

Prizes vary as does the kudos of winning. The Antibes Festival is probably the most prestigious in the underwater film world and definitely worth

a visit.

While Antibes remains the top event in the underwater world, the following list contains details of a number of underwater film festivals that are worth checking out. There are also web sites that will provide updated information – check particularly Christian Redinger's site *www.underwaterfilm.info*

It is always worth expanding the field of your searches and involvement to more general wildlife film festivals and indeed even festivals where all categories of films are welcomed. My list contains only specialised underwater film festivals.

Country	Details
Czech Republic	PAF Tachov – International Diving Festival www.paftachov.cz
France	Antibes Festival Mondial de l'Image Sous Marine www.underwater-festival.com
	Marseilles: CMAS World Championship of Underwater Photography www.imagesub.com
	Strasbourg: Fete de l'Image Sous-Marine fete.image.s.marine.free.fr
	Toulon: Festival International du Film Maritime et d'Exploration www.fifme.com
Italy	Rome: International Underwater Image Festival PE
Malta	Blue Dolphin of Malta International Underwater Photographic Competition
Montenegro	Kotor International Underwater Film Festival Kotor
Russia	Moscow: Moscow International Diving Festival
	Moscow Moscow Video Filming Contest - Black Pearl videodive.ru/indexe.shtml
Serbia	Belgrade International Underwater Film Festival www.kpa.co.yu
Seychelles	SUBIOS www.subios.sc
Slovakia	High Tatras International Festival of Diving Films www.mfpf.sk
Spain	Barcelona Festival Internacional de Imagen Subacuatica www.videosub.org
	Barcelona Setmana Internacional de la Image Submarine www.siisc.com
	San Sebastian Ciclo International de Cine Submarino e-mail subacureal@ixxion.net
Switzerland	Lugano: International Underwater Image Biennial www.biennale-lugano.ch
Turkey	Istanbul International Underwater Photo / Video festival www.armarafestival.com
United Kingdom	UK Image. www.divernet.com
Slovenia	VODAN. hsavodan@arctur.si

A selection of awards and brochures from a number of contests

Arrow crab

11. Travelling

Travelling to collect your footage can be one of the biggest expenses for a film maker. Even if you just take a couple of clean pairs of shorts and T- shirts, the weight of your dive gear and camera equipment will invariably tip the scales well into the realm of excess baggage charges. Rarely a month goes by without one magazine or another publishing letters asking why golfers and other sportsman are exempted from excess baggage charges but divers are not.

This chapter is intended to be a series of tips that I have learnt over the years by trial and error, or lessons that I have picked up from other travelling divers.

What luggage?

My personal luggage is a combination of hard relatively light suitcases such as those in the picture, together with hard equipment cases. Dive gear for myself and my assistant goes in one suitcase, clothing and a housing in the other two, and lights and equipment in the equipment cases. The hard exteriors of both types of case protect the equipment, and spreading the contents judiciously between the several cases means that even if one failed to arrive it would be a nuisance rather than a trip-aborting crisis. The suitcases also have wheels, which is a real bonus. Heavy items can be distributed among the various cases so that no one case exceeds the weight limit per item of any country you may be visiting. Having had the humiliating experience of having to unpack and re-pack the whole of my baggage on the floor in Brisbane Airport to redistribute the weight I can assure you that this is a real bonus.

The shinier and newer the cases the more attractive they are to baggage thieves. Silver cases with an electronics manufacturer's name on them broadcast their contents, while slightly travel weary inconspicuous cases will be ignored. Most of my cases by now are so rusty and beaten up by use that they hardly attract attention.

Many travelling photographers use large cool boxes. These are fairly light when compared to the weight of two ordinary suitcases which is their approximate equivalent carrying capacity. They are solid and robust and can take the roughest of handling. They are relatively cheap to buy when compared to the sometimes ridiculous prices you can pay for more traditional pieces of luggage. They are unlikely to attract the attention of a baggage thief who is far more likely to target an expensive soft-bodied designer label valise than a chunky old and battered cool box – and they are somewhat more conspicuous and less easy to simply walk off with. One well known stills photographer also believes that they are less likely to be ditched by an airline if they are overloaded, as the airline may fear they contain perishables and may result in a claim if delayed.

The only drawbacks with cool boxes as luggage is that the weight of a fully packed cool box and their general shape and size can make them very cumbersome to handle – remember you will not only be checking them in at airports but also having to lug them around for the whole dive trip, in and out of hotels, on buses, and onto dive boats.

It pays to protect your investment. Make sure camera cases have adequate shock absorbtion

Right top: Travel-weary cases
Right: Polystyrene impact protection

Packing

The actual packing of the bags is a matter of common sense. Make sure that there is nothing loose that can rattle around and cause damage to other items or to itself. Use clothing to wrap around fragile items and as padding. At worst, the clothing may get creased but it can always be ironed when you arrive.

Do not pack the cameras in the housings – carry them in your carry-on baggage. Not only are they probably the single most valuable items, but whether a scientifically accepted fact or not I am convinced that the huge drops in temperature in an aircraft hold, coupled with the none-too gentle treatment that checked baggage receives, can do no good at all to sensitive digital cameras.

Take advantage of empty spaces such as the interior of housings – I put my tape stock inside and pad it with small items of clothing.

If packing torches, lights, or anything containing a battery, make absolutely certain that the batteries are disconnected and turned around in the casing so they cannot accidentally get switched on in transit – an item that did so could at the very least irredeemably flatten the battery and at the worst in the confines of a packed case burn itself out and even risk a fire.

If your housing has a pressure release screw ensure it is loosened before flight.

Ensure your baggage is clearly marked in at least two separate places with the full details of your destination, your name and flight numbers. Do not put your home address on the exterior of outbound cases – there can be no clearer advertisement of an empty house with the occupants away. Stick this information on the interior of the lid; if all else fails an airline will eventually break open a case to try and trace its owner and the information will then be easy for them to access.

Excess baggage

This is the dive photographers nightmare. Not only are you carrying full dive gear, but heavy housings, batteries, and electrical equipment, plus and spares! My assistant and I carry a minimum of 140kg between us, and as on many flights the limit per passenger is 20kg. Airports become the nightmare stage of any journey.

Some airlines are 'diver-friendly' and allow divers an extra baggage allowance, but they are still very much in the minority. Check the airline's policies, and if using a travel agent get them to negotiate an extra allowance for you before you confirm your ticket. A good travel agent, particularly one specialising in dive travel, should be able to get at least an extra 10kg for you. Make absolutely sure you have the excess allowance confirmed in writing with the airline's reference number on it. It's amazing how these agreements can't be traced by some awkward check-in clerk unless you can prove it, and your ticket as a standard issue will probably record only the usual 20kg.

There are basically two different sets of rules on excess. Travelling transatlantic and from the USA the limit is two pieces of luggage. Some modify this and limit each bag to 30kg, and rigorously enforce this policy. Flying elsewhere in the world the usual allowance is 20kg.

Airlines will almost invariably allow ten per cent above the allowance; some even as policy don't actually start charging excess until you are substantially more than 10% over.

Friends always offer to come along to help carry your bags, and as a working cameraman, that extra hand can help. On another trip to Asia between two of us we were charged £960 on the outward journey for 30kg excess – a one way charge that came to more than the total cost of the return fares for the two of us! During the trip one housing packed up leaving us about to embark on a 21 day expedition with just one camera. In return for a couple of nights in a Singapore hotel a friend agreed to bring out a replacement housing. The total cost of their trip, including air fares and hotel, was £500 and she took her full allowance of luggage that we could be that stage send home – the result being no excess baggage charge on the return leg.

Info: No mercy, no quarter

On a flight from London to Manila, the airline showed no mercy or leeway, weighing every item including hand baggage, and demanding us £1460 one way. After discussions that included me deciding that I would wear my BC as a waistcoat onto the plane rather than pay their exorbitant demands, the airline compromised at £1,000 – provided I didn't wear my BC! When I wrote on my return complaining, their reply was that if they didn't stick rigidly to their rules, people may take car engines in their baggage. Needless to say I will never again fly that airline. A ticket may look deceptively cheap, but if the airline behaves in this way it can be a false economy.

Golfers and skiers generally get extra baggage allowances despite the awkward shapes of their equipment and the need for special handling, so why are we penalised even though the necessities for our sport and pastime are packed in far easier to handle cases? And the many times I fly on the same airlines with nothing more than an overnight bag do I get a refund? No. I view excess baggage charges as blatant revenue maximisation. 10 kilos of accompanied excess baggage one way London – Singapore costs more than you would expect to pay for a return air fare for a person weighing 100 or more kilos – and that person gets food and drink. So, if the airlines are ripping us off under the pretence of commerciality, I see no reason why I should not try to minimise their ill-gotten gains from me by a few tricks of my own.

Though airlines state that they will allow one item of hand baggage weighing around 6kg, there are certain items that you can get away with in addition. Bags that are clearly camera bags and could not possibly go in the hold are usually allowed as an extra item; laptop computers are also generally allowed on board as a second item and usually have space for a few extra bits and pieces, particularly as though some airlines now weigh carry-on, they never trouble to weigh laptop cases. Ladies handbags can usually have room for a few little extras. And if you have a carrier bag that has clearly come from a shop in the airport it will usually be ignored at check-in as it will be assumed that it just contains a couple of magazines and paperbacks for the journey.

If your official carry-on bag is not too obviously grossly stuffed then often you will get away with it not being weighed – to do this you need to develop the photographer's nonchalant saunter – you have to make the 20kg-plus hanging from each shoulder appear virtually weightless so the check in clerk doesn't challenge you. The other trick involves hiding your carry on behind the nearest pillar where you can keep an eye on them but the check-in clerk can't.

Check in as late as you can – if you arrive early the check-in clerk has the whole shift ahead and all the time in the world. If the gate is about to close they have far less time and inclination to get into arguments and negotiations over excess, and are far more likely to simply rush you through so that the flight boarding is not delayed. It is also worth checking in advance whether it is a full flight when baggage weight checks may be more stringent than a half-full flight.

Don't forget old fashioned courtesy at check in – the clerks always have a degree of discretion and are far more likely to exercise it in favour of someone who is pleasant and friendly to them than an arrogant rude and demanding passenger!

And finally that wonderful invention, the photographer's jacket. Although the initial reaction when seeing someone in a check-in queue may be to wonder what that person is trying to prove, dressing to show the world that he is a photographer, think again – there stands a man wise in the way of evading excess baggage charges. You do not get charged for the weight of your clothing, and the many pockets of that jacket can contain several kilos of the small heavy items such as batteries, spare lenses, and even small weights. It may be a cumbersome item to wear, but as soon as you get on the plane you can stow it in the overhead locker and sit back to enjoy the flight smug in the knowledge of those few extra kilos you haven't had to pay for.

There are less expensive ways of getting baggage to and from a destination than paying excess baggage charges.

Excess baggage charges are calculated as a

percentage of a full published one way economy fare, which may be far more than you actually paid for your ticket from an agent. The rate is generally 3 per cent of the full fare per kilo.

Sending baggage unaccompanied can work out far cheaper – around one third of the excess baggage charges – but there are problems with this course. Firstly the baggage will need to be dispatched several days before you need to collect it to ensure its arrival. It is highly unlikely to arrive on the same flight that you are taking, and certainly if you only check it in on the day you fly, it will rarely if ever arrive at the same time that you do. Secondly, you will need to arrange collection from cargo at the destination and deal with Customs clearance and import duties – often very trying and time consuming particularly if there are language difficulties.

I do not recommend this option for outbound baggage unless you have a long stay at your destination and feel confident about handling procedures at that end. However, if you got hit for excess baggage on the outbound leg of your journey then this option is well worth considering for the return leg when you will not need the baggage so urgently and can deal with the importation

formalities at your leisure on your return.

Another option usually overlooked but very worth considering is an international courier service such as DHL or TNT. Amazingly these may work out even cheaper than unaccompanied baggage, and have the added advantage that they take care of customs clearance and will deliver to your door either at your destination or at your home, usually giving a fairly firm indication of the arrival date. It is also worth considering these services if you have equipment problems or have forgotten something – the service may be far more reasonably priced than you can imagine.

Finally there is the old joke about someone carrying your bags for you though obviously unless that person will be spending their whole stay with you which will incur other expenses, you will have to buy them a return fare to cover the cost of the baggage one way. Even so, depending on the amount to which your baggage exceeds the allowance this can still work to your benefit

So if we meet on some tropical isle or distant dive boat and my tips have helped you reduce your excess baggage liability I'll let you buy me a cold beer.

12. Glossary

Beam angle: This will be expressed in degrees. The standard light will be somewhere between 30 and 60 degrees. For wider-angle work, the wider the beam the better, to avoid a spotlighting effect on the subject. Lights are available on the market with beam angles of up to 110 degrees. For macro work a narrow beam of light is perfectly acceptable.

Burn time: The length of time the battery should keep the light going underwater and is calculated on the basis of leaving the light consistently on until the battery goes flat. I have always found manufacturers burn time figures optimistic – and remember that once the battery starts failing the weaker light will be less use for filming. Burn time also depends on the strength of light you are running from the battery

Charge time: How long it will take to recharge the battery from flat. Often you will be using the lights on a dive trip when you may be making a number of dives each day so this may be an important consideration – quick recharge time can be very convenient – over time I have accumulated a number of different lighting systems that have charging times ranging from three to 18 hours!

Colour absorption: The extent to which the various colour of the spectrum are lost by absorption in the water with depth

Colour Temperature: The measurement of the relative redness or blueness of a light expressed in degrees Kelvin. The higher the Kelvin rating the colder / bluer the light and the lower the Kelvin rating the warmer/redder the light. Video lights usually produce around 3200 - 3400 degrees Kelvin which corresponds with a camera's indoor light setting

Depth of field: The degree to which subjects at differing distances from the camera are in focus. This can range from everything from the camera to infinity being in focus to just subjects within a very limited range

Dimmer: If this facility exists it will either be a fully flexible dimmer or be expressed as for example 50 per cent and 100 per cent, meaning there are two strengths of light available that you can switch between under water.

Dioptre: A magnifying lens screwed onto the camera itself.

Exposure: How wide the aperture of the camera opens thus controlling the amount of light entering each frame of the tape. This works in the same way as the iris in the human eye.

Filter: A coloured transparent lens fitted either to the camera or housing to correct the absorption of specific colours of the spectrum.

Gain: The electronic way to increase the camera's ability to see light and to adjust it's sensitivity to light.

Half-and-half shots: Shots that are partially above water and partially below.

Hot spot: An area on the image where the light is more intense than on the remainder of the image.

Macro: The art of filming the smallest of creatures, or very close-up detail of a larger creature.

Output. This is the strength of the light and is measured in watts. The average light will be 50 watts. 100 watts may be too bright for many uses and lower wattages may be too dim.

Port: The glass or perspex front of a housing through which the camera films

Standard/alternative bulbs: Often appears in a description of a lighting system. This tells you what wattage of bulb comes as standard but also tells you if the light can be adapted by installing a different strength of bulb. This is not something that can be done underwater.

Vignetting: The intrusion of the housing onto the corners of an image.

Weight and displacement: Often appears in a description of a lighting system. These figures are usually supplied separately so you need If the weight exceeds the displacement it will be negatively buoyant. Do your own arithmetic and it will give you a good idea of how the lights will affect the overall buoyancy of your filming rig If you intend travelling by air weight can take on another and expensive significance

White balance: The way of telling the camera what white looks like in any particular lighting situation so that with that point of reference it then knows what other colours should look like by comparison and can automatically adjust accordingly.

White Light: This is sunlight, which of course is composed of all the colours of the spectrum

Zebra function: A function of the camera which will highlight with a zebra pattern any areas of over-lighting in a shot.

Photographic credits

Ian Cartwright pages 78, 79, 86, 88

John Greenamyer pages 4, 7, 8, 10, 14, 16, 18, 52, 59, 60, 66, 67, 80, 81, 85, 90, 94, 95, 96, 107, 116, 122

Matthew Lasky inside cover and pages 5, 13, 30, 35, 43, 61, 63, 73, 75 bottom, 92, 121

Will and Demelza Postlethwaite pages 56,58,77,106

Irvin Rockman pages 42, 70 bottom left and right, 74, 75, 79 top right, 85 bottom, 101 middle right,113, 118 bottom right

Jeremy Stafford-Deitsch page 6

Michele Westmorland page 27

All other images Shark Bay Films

12. Glossary and credits

Notes

Notes